PRAISE FOR *ONE BLOOD*

I am so thankful that John Perkins has written *One Blood*. It is a must-read for all people. John carefully and powerfully weaves Scripture, his personal story, illustrations of true reconciliation with an encouraging style that brings hope. I loved reading it and so will you.

WAYNE GORDON
Founding Pastor of Lawndale Community Church
Chairman of Christian Community Development Association

John Perkins's new book, *One Blood*, is an open invitation for the body of Christ—whether a church, denomination, or individual—to take inventory of our progress. Are we living by Christ's standards, or have we succumbed to those of the world? While the latest research reveals that the average church is stagnant at best, Christ has challenged His church to stay in the race and get His work done! John Perkins's book poses some tough questions and offers practical advice for doing just that.

TONY EVANS
Senior Pastor, Oak Cliff Bible Fellowship
President, The Urban Alternative

This is a powerful, prophetic appeal to people of faith to address our nation's tragic history of racial injustice. Like Daniel, Amos, and Micah, John Perkins has profound insight on the health of our nation and the sin of racial bigotry that has burdened us for too long. *One Blood* is an altar call for justice to which we should all respond.

BRYAN STEVENSON
Founder and executive director of the Equal Justice Initiative, clinical professor at New York University School of Law, and author of *Just Mercy*

I'm not quite sure where to begin with Dr. John Perkins's latest and, perhaps, final book, *One Blood*. I think the best way to capture the heart of this book is that, ultimately, this is a love letter to the church. By this, I'm not suggesting that this is a nebulous or fluffy invitation to a feel good, pop psychology about the injustice of racism. Rather, it's both fierce and tender, pastoral and prophetic, lamenting and hopeful. Dr. Perkins—both through his words and corroborated by a life faithfully lived—invites us to a deeper love for God and for neighbor—including and especially those that don't look like us, think like us, or feel like us. And in a world today of so much pain, fear, and division, we need to desperately be reminded of God's reconciling truth, grace, and love.

EUGENE CHO
Pastor, humanitarian, and author of *Overrated: Are We More in Love with the Idea of Changing the World Than Actually Changing the World?*

One Blood is indeed, in Dr. Perkins's own words, a "manifesto" and the culmination of his life's work and calling to realize biblical reconciliation. There's a clear sense of urgency and candor about the days ahead for the church, the all-important role of the gospel message, and the baton that has to pass to the next generation.

I often say Dr. Perkins is a true national treasure. Here he has written his very heart and soul—a history and biography—in *One Blood*, and has poured all of himself out in beautiful, selfless love. This book is a must-read for any and all who share the burden for this ongoing fight.

JUDAH SMITH
Lead Pastor, Churchome (formerly The City Church)
New York Times bestselling author, *Jesus Is* _____.

John Perkins has been giving me a transfusion of reconciling love for forty years. We may be one, but John has always had the better blood, more of Christ's healing and renewing love. So over and over, both for me and for so many, John has infused us with fresh vision and bold passion for God's reconciling love and justice. This wise book testifies that that same blood is still vital and pumping hard!

MARK LABBERTON
President, Fuller Theological Seminary

PARTING
WORDS
TO THE
CHURCH
ON RACE
AND LOVE

ONE
BLOOD

JOHN M. PERKINS

WITH KAREN WADDLES

MOODY PUBLISHERS

CHICAGO

All Scripture quotations, unless otherwise indicated, are taken from the New American Standard Bible®, Copyright © 1960, 1962, 1963, 1968, 1971, 1972, 1973, 1975, 1977, 1995 by The Lockman Foundation. Used by permission. (www.Lockman.org)

Scripture quotations marked NLT are taken from the Holy Bible, New Living Translation, copyright © 1996, 2004, 2007, 2013 by Tyndale House Foundation. Used by permission of Tyndale House Publishers, Inc., Carol Stream, Illinois 60188. All rights reserved.

Scripture quotations marked KJV are taken from the King James Version.

Scripture quotations marked NIV are taken from the Holy Bible, New International Version®, NIV®. Copyright © 1973, 1978, 1984, 2011 by Biblica, Inc.™ Used by permission of Zondervan. All rights reserved worldwide. www.zondervan.com. The "NIV" and "New International Version" are trademarks registered in the United States Patent and Trademark Office by Biblica, Inc.™

Scripture quotations marked ISV are taken from *The Holy Bible: International Standard Version*. Release 2.0, Build 2015.02.09. Copyright © 1995-2014 by ISV Foundation. ALL RIGHTS RESERVED INTERNATIONALLY. Used by permission of Davidson Press, LLC.

Scripture quotations marked NCV are taken from the New Century Version®. Copyright © 2005 by Thomas Nelson. Used by permission. All rights reserved.

Scripture quotations marked MSG are taken from THE MESSAGE, copyright © 1993, 1994, 1995, 1996, 2000, 2001, 2002 by Eugene H. Peterson. Used by permission of NavPress. All rights reserved. Represented by Tyndale House Publishers, Inc.

Scripture quotations marked CEV are from the Contemporary English Version Copyright © 1991, 1992, 1995 by American Bible Society. Used by Permission.

Edited by Elizabeth Cody Newenhuyse
Interior and cover design: Erik M. Peterson
Author photo: Will Sterling, Sterling Photography

Library of Congress Cataloging-in-Publication Data

Names: Perkins, John, 1930- author.
Title: One blood : parting words to the church on race and love / John Perkins.
Other titles: Parting words to the church on race
Description: Chicago : Moody Publishers, 2018. | Includes bibliographical references.
Identifiers: LCCN 2017056585 (print) | LCCN 2018016301 (ebook) | ISBN 9780802495501 (ebook) | ISBN 9780802418012
Subjects: LCSH: United States--Race relations. | Racism--United States--Psychological aspects. | Racism--Religious aspects--Christianity. | Civil rights--Religious aspects--Christianity. | Race relations--Religious aspects--Christianity. | Reconciliation. | Church and social problems--United States.
Classification: LCC E185.615 (ebook) | LCC E185.615 .P424 2018 (print) | DDC 305.800973--dc23
LC record available at https://lccn.loc.gov/2017056585

ISBN 978-0-8024-1801-2

We hope you enjoy this book from Moody Publishers. Our goal is to provide high-quality, thought-provoking books and products that connect truth to your real needs and challenges. For more information on other books and products written and produced from a biblical perspective, go to www.moodypublishers.com or write to:

Moody Publishers
820 North LaSalle Boulevard
Chicago, IL 60610

3 5 7 9 10 8 6 4 2

Printed in the United States of America

To my soulmate, Vera Mae, whose love has inspired and sustained me; and to my grandchildren (Johnathan Spencer, Rebekah Jubilee, April Joy, Varah Aleya, Karah Spencer, Toneasha Slater, John Phillip, David Wilson, Peydria Alene, John Michael, Shelby Karyssa, John Wayne, and Ashley) and great-grandchildren (Khalil Parker, John Phillip Jr., Sarah Patrice, Jonathan Carey, DaSean Quincy, Charli Eden, Kynli Nichole, and Eva), who must take up the mantle and run your own race. May you always seek His good pleasure.

CONTENTS

Foreword • 9

Introduction • 15

1 The Church Should Look Like That • 27
2 One Race, One Blood • 43
LIVING IT OUT: Mosaic Church, Little Rock • 58

3 A Lament for Our Broken Past • 63
4 The Healing Balm of Confession • 79
LIVING IT OUT: Fellowship Church, Monrovia, California • 94

5 Forgiveness: It's in Our DNA • 99
6 Tear Down This Wall! • 113
LIVING IT OUT: Water of Life Community Church, Fontana, California • 128

7 God Don't Want No Coward Soldiers • 131
8 Prayer, the Weapon of Our Warfare • 145
LIVING IT OUT: Epiphany Fellowship, Philadelphia • 158

9 The Greatest of These Is Love • 161
EPILOGUE: Almost Home • 171

Afterword • 177
Study Guide • 181
Contributing Pastors • 189
Notes • 193
Acknowledgments • 199
About the Authors • 201

FOREWORD

At eighty-seven years old, my dear friend John Perkins is near to the end of his journey here on earth. He has lived a life of ministry dedicated to the cause of reconciliation. He has literally inspired thousands of people to live out their lives in service of the gospel through evangelism and community development. All of us who have been privileged to be in fellowship and work alongside him know that John is a prophet of God in our time. He is truly a great man.

This "greatness" has come from his single-minded perseverance to the gospel through which, in over six decades of ministry, he has gained more wisdom than most. He could look back and provide us some important lessons from his successes and failures. However, he has chosen to do something more important. John writes deeply about his recognition that the problems of reconciliation we face in our country, indeed the whole world, are

> much too big to be wrestled to the ground by plans that begin in the minds of men. This is a God-sized problem. It is one that only the Church, through the power of the Holy Spirit, can heal. It requires the quality of love that only our Savior can provide.

John Perkins is calling the Church to be the Church. He is echoing the message of God's restorative work on our behalf and reminding us, pleading with us, to be reconcilers.

God . . . reconciled us to Himself through Christ and gave us the ministry of reconciliation. (2 Cor. 5:18)

I am both saddened and encouraged that John has subtitled this book as his "parting words to the Church on race and love." I am saddened because I don't want him to "depart." I want him to continue admonishing and teaching us, to continue imparting the wisdom that comes from ministry in the trenches. I have so much to learn from this saint. I want to hear more. Among Christ's last recorded words is the command to "go and make disciples of all nations" (Matt. 28:19 NIV).

They are powerful and meaningful because He knew He had little time left with His disciples and He didn't want to waste it on trivial conversation. He shared with them the most important things. I hope and pray John Perkins is with us for many years, but in this last season of ministry, he is burdened with this message to us, the Church. It is important; it is not trivial. John calls it his manifesto. We must listen!

I am encouraged because he sees, as do I, that the Church is the hope of the world. If we are to have any meaning, dare I say "purpose," we must understand what God is asking us to be and do. In the midst of all the pain, oppression, and lack of meaning in life, the Church must proclaim the answer that is provided to us so clearly in Scripture. It is simple. We must be loving like Jesus in this fractured world.

As John reminds us with his life and through his many books, we must start with ourselves. We must also acknowledge the lack of true reconciliation experienced in our church life. If the church is truly the hope of the world, and I believe this with all my heart, reconciliation must be our lifestyle. So, how do we do this?

We must treat every person with **dignity**. As Scripture says,

Live as free people, but do not use your freedom as an excuse to do evil. Live as servants of God. Treat everyone you meet with dignity. Love your spiritual family. Revere God. Respect the government. (1 Peter 2:16–17 NCV/MSG)

This is hard to do in a world that has become more polarized, angrier, more divisive. John has been beaten, spit upon, and oppressed simply for being black. Yet, he has chosen, as must we all, to treat people with dignity. We know that God created us with dignity.

You have made them [people] a little lower than the angels and crowned them with glory and honor. (Ps. 8:5 NIV)

Our Declaration of Independence affirms Scripture in that "We hold these truths to be self-evident, that all men are created equal, that they are endowed by their Creator with certain unalienable Rights."

John is correct when he asserts we can't "give" people dignity, we can only *affirm* it. Dignity comes from God, and God has already given it to everyone when He created us in His image, sent Jesus to die for us, and put His Holy Spirit inside of us. We just affirm people's dignity by treating them with the respect they deserve.

At the same time, we acknowledge that God intentionally created everyone to be **unique.** I know no better way to illustrate this than through what the Scriptures tell us:

God gives everything the kind of body he wants it to have. (1 Cor. 15:38 CEV)

"From one man [Adam] he [God] made all the nations ...

11

and he marked out their appointed times in history and the boundaries of their lands." (Acts 17:26 NIV)

In almost all cultures, we are naturally taught to distrust what is different. We're tribal, and we feel most comfortable with people like ourselves. That is not God's intention. God wanted us all to be His family. He wants us to live in **community**. We need each other and we are better together.

The mystery of Christ . . . was not made known to people in other generations as it has now been revealed by the Spirit to God's holy apostles and prophets. This mystery is that through the gospel the Gentiles are heirs together with Israel, members together of one body, and sharers together in the promise in Christ Jesus. (Eph. 3:4–6 NIV)

The title of this book is *One Blood*. As John has said, racism makes an assumption that there is more than one race. But Scripture is clear: we are all a part of the human race, and the path to being family is the path of forgiveness and love. God has incarnated Himself so we could have the forgiveness of sin. Our first task in building the community God has made us for is to forgive and love each other. If you don't have the right relationships, you won't have the right identity. That's why the Scripture stresses that we're made to be one in Christ, and we're formed for God's family. God's secret plan is no longer a secret!

Have you ever wondered why God didn't just create us and then immediately take us to heaven? Why does He have us spend time on earth first? The answer is: we were put on earth to learn how to **love!** Jesus said,

"So now I am giving you a new commandment: Love each

other. Just as I have loved you, you should love each other. Your love for one another will prove to the world that you are my disciples." (John 13:34–35 NLT)

Keep on loving each other as brothers and sisters. (Heb. 13:1 NCV)

I have often heard my friend John say, "You can't find any end in the depths of love!" This is from a man who experienced visceral hate. Yet, because he knows how deeply God loves him, he learned to love others, even those who hated him. We can too. In fact, we MUST learn this! It is commanded by Jesus. It is how we become like Him.

How do you specifically love somebody who's different from you? First, by listening to them. When you listen to somebody, you're loving them. Your ears are your greatest tool for love. Then look at them. When you look people in the eye, when you give them your total attention, you are showing love. Then learn from them. You can learn from anybody if you know the right questions to ask. And laugh with them! Humor is a great barrier breaker. It builds bridges. Laughter is the gift of love. If you listen, look, learn, and laugh with others, you will learn to love.

Treating people with dignity; accepting and celebrating our uniqueness; forgiving each other and being in community; and learning to love like Jesus are all part of what God wants us to learn while we're here on earth. The Bible says that we have been given "the ministry of reconciliation" (2 Cor. 5:18). This is our calling, and our broken, fractured world desperately needs it!

If we're not helping people reconcile, we're not the church!

13

Saddleback Church was built on ten values, one for each letter of our name. The A in S.A.D.D.L.E.B.A.C.K. stands for "All nation congregation." In other words, we are intentionally a multiethnic church. We say "we want our church to look like heaven is going to look," and we feel like we are making progress—our members speak sixty-seven different languages! Saddleback may be one of the most ethnically diverse churches in America because for thirty-eight years, it has been a stated value of our congregation. That diversity is one of the keys to its strength and success.

As a pastor who has heard countless people utter their last words, I know that last words are important. So I urge you to pay attention to John Perkins's "parting words to the Church on race and love." Let's act on this message that comes straight from Scripture by being the church that brings hope to a broken world. Let us work and pray that through the power of the Holy Spirit the vision of John the apostle in Revelation 7:9 will come to pass quickly:

After this I looked, and there before me was a great multitude that no one could count, from every nation, tribe, people and language, standing before the throne and before the Lamb. (NIV)

—**RICK WARREN**
Founding pastor of Saddleback Church
Author of *The Purpose Driven Life*

INTRODUCTION

*But you, be sober in all things, endure hardship, do the work of
an evangelist, fulfill your ministry. For I am already being poured out
as a drink offering, and the time of my departure has come.*

—2 TIMOTHY 4:5–6

I'm eighty-seven years old. I've lived a long life, and I'm full
of gratitude for the opportunities that I've had to serve a
wise, merciful, almighty God. I'm continually in awe of how
far He has brought me, a poor boy from Mississippi with only
a third-grade education.

I grew up in a sharecropping family in Mississippi and
dropped out of school between the third and fifth grade. Yet,
by God's grace, I've lectured at world-renowned universities
and received honorary doctorates.

My older brother Clyde, who served his country in the
Army in World War II, was shot and killed by a deputy mar-
shal soon after returning home. I have been spat upon and
brutally beaten by police. Yet, by God's grace, I've worked
tirelessly to help build good relations between local police
and urban communities.

I've ministered in country towns, inner cities, and before
large crowds. I've traveled across Europe, Asia, Africa, and
Latin America. I've had the privilege of teaching wide-eyed
emerging leaders as well as foggy-eyed accomplished pioneers.

All of this . . . by His amazing grace.

For more than sixty-five years, I've known the love of a wonderful woman. Together, Vera Mae and I have raised and loved eight children, thirteen grandkids, and eight great-grandkids. We've witnessed the miracle of birth, but also experienced the pain of losing our oldest and youngest sons.

At my age, I'm thankful to God for a mind sharp enough to keep studying His Word. But like a butcher's knife, I know that repeated use means the blade will eventually become dull. I'll try not to be dull here.

I've given most of my life to the cause of reconciliation, fighting the battle in the trenches, and working with community development organizations. We developed the 3 Rs—relocation, reconciliation, and redistribution—to offer a process to help communities work together to balance some of the inequities of life in America. By God's grace, much good work has been done; and I'm humbled to have been a part of it.

But as I come closer to the end of my journey, I am aware that community development can only take us so far—because this is a gospel issue. The problem of reconciliation in our country and in our churches is much too big to be wrestled to the ground by plans that begin in the minds of men. This is a God-sized problem. It is one that only the Church, through the power of the Holy Spirit, can heal. It requires the quality of love that only our Savior can provide. And it requires that we make some uncomfortable confessions. G. K. Chesterton said, "It isn't that they can't see the solution. It is that they can't see the problem." I believe this statement can be applied to the lack of reconciliation within the Church today. We've not been able to arrive at the solution because we haven't seen or acknowledged the problem.

The problem is that there is a gaping hole in our gospel. We have preached a gospel that leaves us believing that we can be reconciled to God but not reconciled to our Christian brothers and sisters who don't look like us—brothers and sisters with whom we are, in fact, one blood.

The apostle John talks about that: "If someone says, 'I love God,' and hates his brother, he is a liar; for the one who does not love his brother whom he has seen, cannot love God whom he has not seen" (1 John 4:20). We've taken out these key parts: reconciliation and the requirement for justice, essential and crucial parts of the gospel. For most of my life I have been working hard to help us fill in this deep, gaping hole by insisting that we admit to some hard truths.

From our early days as a country we adopted the practice of slavery and demonized the slave as inferior, subhuman, and deserving of exploitation. For this wicked system of slavery to survive there had to be distinctions made between normal folks and this new breed of people that would be treated like animals. This is where the idea of race came into play. The truth is that there is no black race—and there is no white race. So the idea of "racial reconciliation" is a false idea. It's a lie. It implies that there is more than one race. This is absolutely false. God created only one race—the human race. We will talk more about this later; but for the purposes of our discussion in this book, I will not use the term "racial reconciliation" but will instead use multiethnic reconciliation, biblical reconciliation, or unity because they more closely describe what we're trying to accomplish. Biblical reconciliation is *the removal of tension between parties and the restoration of loving relationship.*

Many of us have struggled with the big question of how to

make lasting strides in the area of biblical reconciliation. As I look back on a life that has been devoted to this great mystery, I want to try to offer us a path back. Not back to our history that has been littered with missteps and misguided notions, but a path back to what God intended for His church. A path back to the experience of Pentecost, when people from all over the known world heard the glorious message of salvation in their own language. That was reconciliation at its very best. And it's a beautiful picture.

As you read this book I hope that you are able to hear His tender voice speaking through me. We'll talk about race in our country, our history as a nation, and our role as the church in all of it.

We're at a unique moment in our history. We've come through—and in many ways are still in the midst of—great upheaval. The soul of our nation has been laid bare. When I talk to people all over the country it seems like everyone is looking for an answer. There is confusion and way too much anger. I'm grateful that new conversations are beginning to take place; and the right questions are finally being asked. There are some generational batons being passed. This is a crucial moment.

I am reminded of the inaugural address of John F. Kennedy, as the youngest person elected as president of the United States. He said these words: "Let the word go forth from this time and place, to friend and foe alike, that the torch has been passed to a new generation of Americans." I believe that we're at another one of those moments now. As I travel across the country and visit one multiethnic church after another, I see some new warriors who are ready to take up the mantle and run with it. My prayer is that this book becomes for them a resource that will help light the way.

I'd like to think of this as a manifesto of sorts. The word *manifesto* might sound dogmatic or self-important, but it's the word I keep coming back to when I think of what I want to accomplish with this book. One definition of *manifesto* describes it as "a written statement declaring publicly the intentions, motives, or views of its issuer." Another calls it "a public written declaration of principles, policies, and objectives." My personal definition falls somewhere in between. The message found in these pages could be my most personal yet; however, it is also my most earnest attempt to put down in writing the principles I believe to be vital to a complete ministry of reconciliation.

We'll begin in chapter 1: "The Church Should Look Like That" with a look at God's vision for the church. We'll look at that grand heavenly vision of Revelation 7 and argue that God never intended for His body to be one group that all looked the same. From the beginning of Scripture to the end, the message of unity and diversity in the family of God is powerful. Unity was sown into the very fabric of creation: from one man, Adam, all of mankind was created.

But this unity was to be reflected through great diversity. There are hints of the vision sprinkled through the Old Testament, signs that God was going to graft outsiders into His family, creating a multicolored body. God was beginning to graft in outsiders like Ruth, Rahab, and others to show that though the people of Israel were His chosen people, He intended to spread the tent far and wide—that He intended to make, out of many peoples, one family of God.

I'll suggest that issues of justice, diversity, and reconciliation are not extra add-ons that the church can opt out of as a matter of personal preference. They are an essential part of the gospel.

The gospel was first delivered to a multicultural first-century audience (see Acts 2). And the expectation since then has been that it would be distributed and shared widely "to the ends of the earth," and that our strategic plan would be to "make disciples of all nations" (see Matt. 28).

In chapter 2: "One Race, One Blood," we'll discuss the glorious truth that God only created one race. This chapter will challenge our biases and prejudices and help us understand how we got here. Most of us are familiar with the Human Genome Project. Scientists set out to understand the human gene. What they discovered was that every human being is 99.9 percent identical in genetic makeup. What that means is that all the differences that we can see only amount to .1 percent of our genes. Even scientists have proven that we are one.

We've drawn the title of this book from this truth in both the physical and spiritual realms. Just as from one man, Adam, all human physical life began, it is from the blood of one man, Jesus, that all who believe in Him are born again and united into the family of God. We are indeed One Race . . . One Blood.

The concept of the black race and the white race originated with the Enemy himself. Just as he sowed the seeds of doubt in the garden of Eden with his "hath God really said," he has continued through the ages to offer a lie in the place of God's truth. His attack has been anything but subtle. This web of deceit has brought hatred and bigotry into the church. What we are left with is a huge divide that is no more evident than at the 11:00 worship hour on Sunday mornings. We are a divided body. We'll ask Him to give us new eyes to see one another—not as black or white, but as brother and sister in Christ. This is a challenge to reject the "I don't see color" ar-

gument and to embrace the diversity that we see in each other
as an essential part of our oneness.

In chapter 3: "A Lament for Our Broken Past," we'll offer
lament as a crucial part of the journey back to His vision
for His church. In Old Testament times the people of God
mourned and grieved when they realized that they had fallen
short of God's commands. Again and again we see the prophets of old challenging Israel with God's words of judgment,
and we see the people cry out to God for healing and forgiveness. I believe strongly that the church in America has
much to lament: our separation because of race, our misuse of
Scripture to justify the ugly system of slavery, the multitude
of missed opportunities for the kingdom, our shortsighted
vision concerning social justice and the gospel, our misdirected mission effort, and finally our lack of contrition for our
collective sin.

This is an unpopular message today, but I believe it is
appropriate for us to lament as individuals and as the body of
Christ for our mishandling of the vision. I will close out this
chapter with my own personal lament for where we are today
in light of His awesome vision. As I reflect back, I realize that
there were times when I allowed fear to prevent me from
telling all of the hard truth. When others didn't want to hear it
I could have been bolder in pressing forward.

In chapter 4: "The Healing Balm of Confession," we'll talk
about how important it is for confession to take place on an
individual level and on the Church and denominational level.
We'll discuss how this can help us find healing in the places
where we are broken. Both the parable of the prodigal son
and Paul and Silas's encounter with the Philippian jailer offer
powerful insights into how confession and mutual brokenness

can move us forward on this journey to reconciliation.

We'll talk about black anger, white privilege, and mutual fear. And we will offer a picture of how we can each wash the other's wounds. We'll have some honest conversation about how we have fallen short in representing the oneness and unity Scripture demands. I am especially encouraged to see that there has been some movement in the arena of confession on the part of some key denominations recently. We'll celebrate what God is doing.

We can't really talk about lament and confession without spending time in the neighborhood of forgiveness. Chapter 5: "Forgiveness: It's in Our DNA," will present some compelling examples of forgiveness that will give us courage to take a chance. Risk a change of heart. Dare to reach across the divide in meaningful ways to move the discussion beyond feelings of anger and hurt. Much can be learned from the shootings at the Emanuel African Methodist Episcopal Church in Charleston, South Carolina, the shootings at the Amish school in Lancaster County, Pennsylvania, and from the Truth and Reconciliation Commission that was formed after apartheid was broken in South Africa.

We'll be reminded that forgiveness is in agreement with the character of our God. We look like Him when we forgive. It is at that precise moment that the watching world gets a glimpse of Him. This glimpse has the potential to draw all men unto Him. What is at stake when the church forgives is His reputation and His name in this world. I'm hopeful that we can see how crucial this is for each of us individually, for the church collectively, and for His ultimate kingdom purposes.

In chapter 6: "Tear Down This Wall!" we'll discuss in very practical ways what repentance looks like. This is the place where we will be challenged to move from principle to practice—to put our feet to the metal and move in a different direction. Repentance means a change of mind about an action, and it requires an opposite response. We'll offer some suggestions for how that might look in the area of reconciliation—as individuals and as local churches.

Our culture has seemingly lost the grace of a smile and a friendly greeting. We'll talk about that. We'll discuss the importance of knowing a person's name and how that can move us along on this journey to reconciliation. And we'll challenge the notion of gentrification and argue that individuals and churches that choose to remain in ethnically changing neighborhoods are models of what Jesus would do.

In chapter 7: "God Don't Want No Coward Soldiers," we'll discuss commitment and dedication. We simply cannot do the hard work of reconciliation without great commitment. This work is hard, and the forces of evil are engaged to prevent it from happening. There have been some giants who walked before us and have shown us the way. We can learn much from them. They now stand among that great cloud of witnesses who urge us onward and upward. I want to share some of their stories with you. They were heroes because they were willing to risk their lives and all that they had for the cause of reconciliation. As dark as much of our history is, God has also given us moments of great light, and I want to highlight some of those moments.

In chapter 8: "Prayer, the Weapon of Our Warfare," we'll suggest that what we're engaging in—if we are serious about pleasing the Lord—is nothing less than spiritual warfare. We dare not try to fight this fight with man-made ideas and solutions. That's what we've used for generations, and it has not worked. We will be challenged to use prayer as the key weapon in this fight.

Those of us who have fought for reconciliation have often been labeled as people who are all about doing and not enough praying. If we are going to see God's will done and the Church come together as one, it will not happen without believing prayer. Prayer is the foundation for anything that honors God.

And finally, in chapter 9: "The Greatest of These Is Love," we'll highlight the character of Christ in us as the answer to this dilemma. I am in awe of His love that would choose to use someone like me in this great work. His love has been a constant companion and has overflowed through my heart to family, friend, and foe. My deep gratitude to Him would not let me choose to withhold love. There is no power greater than love. It can break down the walls of prejudice and hate that we struggle with.

Along the way we'll call attention to the many bright examples of multiethnic congregations and ministries around our nation that are going against the grain to bring diverse people together. We're calling these features "Living It Out." We'll challenge the church to make that the norm in our churches today, to live out the vision of "one blood." We've asked the leaders of these churches to share their process in becoming multicultural.

These churches and ministries give me so much hope. And I'm thankful to God that as I look out into the horizon I still have hope. I can identify with Martin Luther King Jr. when he said, "I might not get to the Promised Land with you, but I believe that we'll get there." I can see it.

Some of what I need to say may be hard to hear. I understand that. Allow me the privilege of an elder statesman. It used to be in our communities that when the elders spoke, people listened. They didn't have to sugarcoat everything and make it sound pretty. Their advanced years afforded them a platform to be heard and respected. I hope you'll allow me that privilege. And I hope you'll understand that everything I say is because of a deep love for the church, the bride of Christ, and for every human being who is marked by His image.

In many ways this is a short book about everything I want the church to know before I leave this place. You can have a conversation with a person, talking for hours, but it seems like the last words are what finally speak from their heart. Last words are important. There's an urgency about them. But the urgency is not only on my account. We have only to look at the signs of the times to realize that the Church may not have long to get this right. We may not have much time left to offer the world a glimpse of this unity that will point the eyes of the watching world to the power of our great God. Yes, there's an urgency. Time is running out . . . for *all* of us. But while we still have time, let's reflect on the heart of Jesus, who prayed earnestly that His church might one day be one. This is what I want you—*the church*—to know. This is my manifesto.

THE CHURCH SHOULD LOOK LIKE THAT

After these things I looked, and behold, a great multitude which no one could count, from every nation and all tribes and peoples and tongues, standing before the throne and before the Lamb, clothed in white robes, and palm branches were in their hands; and they cry out with a loud voice, saying, "Salvation to our God who sits on the throne, and to the Lamb." —REVELATION 7:9-10

A short time ago we worshiped with the Bridgeway Community Church in Columbia, Maryland. I got a foretaste of this Revelation 7 vision. It felt like a prelude to heaven! It was a picture of the oneness and the diversity of the body of Christ . . . a physical representation of, as the King James Version puts it, "all nations, and kindreds, and people, and tongues," and it was glorious! The melting of the cultures was beautiful; the blend of ethnicities was evident across the ranks of the leadership and the membership. And the music carried me away. I saw echoes of that great congregation that will stand around the throne shouting "Holy, Holy, Holy! Worthy is the Lamb!"

I was struck by their wonderful application of biblical truth. They had been intentional in making sure that their church looked like what the church is supposed to look like. From the Lobby Crew who wore purple T-shirts that ask people in different languages "got questions?" to the warm welcome, "We're so glad you're here today," we saw and felt the heart of this community of believers. What is happening at Bridgeway Community Church and many other multicultural churches across the country is a reflection of God's grand vision for His church. This is a picture of true biblical reconciliation—*the removal of tension between parties and the restoration of loving relationship.* These are glimpses of heaven in our midst.

GOOD NEWS FOR ALL

This vision for unity is borne on the wings of the good news of the gospel. It's good news and it's for all the people. It's the good news that Luke proclaimed, "Do not be afraid; for behold, I bring you good news of great joy which will be for all the people; for today in the city of David there has been born for you a Savior, who is Christ the Lord" (Luke 2:10–11). This supernatural announcement is one of the most compelling signs that God intends for His gospel to reach all nations and cultures.

That the angel would appear to make this announcement of Jesus' birth is big news by itself, but that this angel would choose shepherds in the fields as his target audience is even more noteworthy. This is significant for at least a couple of reasons. First, some say the shepherds in this culture would have been considered "outcasts of society," occupying a lower rung on the class ladder of the day. Some suggest that these shepherds would have been separated from others in the Jewish community because of their inability to follow the Mosaic laws of cleanliness due to their dirty jobs. This would be right in line with the arrival of a Messiah who later would clearly identify with the "least of these" in society.

And there are still other ideas about why God chose these shepherds to receive the good news of Jesus' coming. According to one scholar, the flocks of sheep at the location where these shepherds worked were likely reserved for sacrifice at the temple. So these shepherds had to keep their flocks safe from blemish or harm since their sheep would be used for temple sacrifice. If this was the case, then these were no ordinary shepherds. They were people who understood the importance of a sacrificial lamb in a very intimate and direct way.

Then the angel said, "I bring you good news of great joy." This was something the world had been waiting for since Adam and Eve sinned in the garden of Eden. Death, violent crime, and wickedness had entered into the world. Mankind's nature had moved from constant communion with God to the practice of greed and self-preservation. Satan had done a job on us with the fall. We knew we were messed up, but we couldn't stop ourselves from doing wrong. Only God could do that. And so we began to anticipate a time when God would make things right and return us to a state of harmony with Him.

The angel brought "good news." This had been the greatest longing in human history. And this was going to be the answer to man's long dilemma. "Behold, I bring you good news of great joy which will be for all the people."

Now, hold on for a moment and ponder those last four words: "for all the people."

This was not going to be an exclusive club that continued the then (as now) very common injustice of the "haves" and the "have-nots." This wasn't a message for some and not for others. This was good news for *everyone*—for every man, woman, and child of every nation and culture. There was no room for racism or bigotry. God's plan was too tight.

It's a justice statement: "Behold, I bring you good news of great joy which will be for all the people. For today in the city of David there has been born for you a Savior, who is Christ the Lord."

And it's not just a message for a select few. It's a word of hope and reconciliation "for all the people."

AMERICA'S BROKEN GOSPEL

The angel's message was good news for the world, but it's especially good news for those of us in America—not because we're better than anyone else, but because our founding documents were in line with the angel's inclusive message.

I believe the Declaration of Independence makes the greatest affirmative statement about reconciliation in human history. There has not been a statement before or since that was more comprehensive than our great Declaration of Independence, our creed: "We hold these truths to be self-evident, that all men are created equal, that they are endowed by their Creator with certain unalienable Rights, that among these are Life, Liberty and the pursuit of Happiness."[1]

"We hold these truths to be self-evident ... all men are created equal ..." You can't be any more truthful than that. That's one of the greatest statements in human history, because we were created in the image of God.

America was unique, because it was directly drawing on

this divine right of humanity, over and above any kind of class system set up by man against man. All people are created equal! (The irony that this great vision for equality was put forth by a group of men who owned other human beings as property was an obvious flaw in the plan—but just go along with me for now.)

America was different from the start. We were going to be a nation that reflected the divine values of God's kingdom, one nation from all nations under heaven, under God. We'd live together. We'd work together. We'd govern as a united people, each with an equally valid voice.

But then we got sidetracked. Our personal interests took priority over the equality of other human beings. We decided we valued individualism more than community. We determined that, despite the God-honoring ideals of our founding statement, we each needed to get ours first. And then it all fell apart.

We've been longing for the fulfillment of that founding vision ever since. We've had a few fleeting gestures to try to go there. We had the Civil War. We had the Civil Rights movement. We passed laws and launched programs. But we haven't been able to pull it together.

The angel told the shepherds, "Behold, I bring you good news."

That was a message for the world, but it was a message entrusted *to God's people.*

I tell you, the church has got to do it. The people of God have got to do it.

THE MANDATE FOR UNITY

But for the message of the gospel to truly have power, the people of God must deliver the news as one united body. This good news was to be delivered to the world by a *multicultural, united* body of believers—the Church. The Church has been given a divine mandate for reconciliation. Our Lord Jesus Christ before He went to Calvary prayed a prayer that helps us see and know how important this vision of oneness, of reconciliation, is to God. After praying that the Father would glorify Him and praying for His disciples, He prayed for "those who [will] believe in Me through their word" (John 17:20; also see 2 Cor. 5:18–21). That's you and me. He prayed

> *"that they may all be one; even as You, Father, are in Me, and I in You, that they also may be in Us, so that the world may believe that You sent Me. The glory which You have given Me I have given to them, that they may be one just as We are one; I in them and You in Me, that they may be perfected in unity, so that the world may know that You sent Me and loved them, even as You have loved Me."*
> *(John 17:21–23)*

For too long, many in the Church have argued that unity in the body of Christ across ethnic and class lines is a separate issue from the gospel. There has been the suggestion that we can be reconciled to God without being reconciled to our brothers and sisters in Christ. Scripture doesn't bear that out. We only need to examine what happened when the Church was birthed to see exactly how God intends for this issue of reconciliation within the body of Christ to fall out. In the book of Acts we begin to see what happens when God's radical vision for the

Church collides with the culture. Man is sinful and does not easily give up his prejudices and dislikes. But again and again the Holy Spirit had His way and wrestled the people of God to submission on this issue of reconciliation.

The apostle Peter struggled with the vision of reconciliation. He was steeped in Jewish culture, which had taught him to see non-Jews as unclean. But God opened his eyes to a new truth when Peter fell into a trance. In this trance, he saw the heavens open and something like a great sheet being let down by its four corners upon the earth. In it were all kinds of animals and reptiles and birds of the air. These were clean and unclean animals, according to Jewish law! All mixed up together. And suddenly a voice spoke to him saying, "Get up, Peter, kill and eat" (Acts 10:13).

You can just imagine how insulted Peter was to hear these words! He understood that it was the Lord speaking, yet he said, "No, Lord." Somewhere along the way, I've heard it said that you can't say, "No" and "Lord" in the same sentence. They just don't go together. If He is Lord, then He is Ruler and Commander. So the Lord tells Peter once again not to call what He has made unclean or common. This happened three times, but Peter was still confused about the vision.

I can identify with Peter. It's taken a long time for me to really understand how crucial it is for the Church to be united. I've worked at the issue of reconciliation from the outside and I've worked with black churches and white churches. And I'm just now seeing clearly that the black church can't fix this. And the white church can't fix this. It must be the reconciled Church, black and white Christians together imaging Christ to the world.

It wasn't until messengers from Cornelius's house came to

find him and take him to see Cornelius that Peter began to see the vision for true biblical reconciliation opening up before his very eyes. He found himself in the home of a Gentile. Some of his first words to Cornelius were, "You yourselves know how unlawful it is for a man who is a Jew to associate with a foreigner or to visit him; and yet God has shown me that I should not call any man unholy or unclean" (Acts 10:28). Remember these words. We will revisit them later.

Yes, Peter was finally beginning to understand that loving God meant loving even our enemies—loving those we have previously hated. Can you hear the passion in his voice when he proclaimed, "I most certainly understand now that God is not one to show partiality, but in every nation the man who fears Him and does what is right is welcome to Him" (vv. 34–35)?

I imagine that not even Peter had any idea of just how far God was going to go to demonstrate that He is not a respecter of persons. He was not going to have a Jewish church and a separate Gentile church of second-class believers. Because when Peter preached the good news to Cornelius and his family, the Holy Spirit fell on all of them. The Gentiles began speaking in tongues and praising God! It was a repeat of Pentecost!

This was the vision! *All* people, *all* kindred, *all* nations, *all* tongues. One blood. But it was the vision realized when Peter accepted the mandate to love those he had been taught to hate. This was true biblical reconciliation and the demonstration of this biblical truth:

> *For He Himself is our peace, who made both groups into one and broke down the barrier of the dividing wall, by abolishing in His flesh the enmity, which is the Law of*

commandments contained in ordinances, so that in Himself He might make the two into one new man, thus establishing peace, and might reconcile them both in one body to God through the cross, by it having put to death the enmity. (Eph. 2:14–16)

The first church in Acts got it right too. They learned that God's love required them to widen the net and embrace those who were considered outsiders before. How could they not? When the fire of Pentecost ushered in the abiding presence of the Holy Spirit, they all heard the gospel in their own tongue: "Parthians and Medes and Elamites, and residents of Mesopotamia, Judea and Cappadocia, Pontus and Asia, Phrygia and Pamphylia, Egypt and the districts of Libya around Cyrene, and visitors from Rome, both Jews and proselytes, Cretans and Arabs" (Acts 2:9–11a). It was clear that God intended for His church to be made up of many different people groups, not just those of the Jewish faith.

The church in Acts saw the urgent need to deal with any hint of ethnic superiority. When the Greek-speaking Jewish widows complained that they were not receiving the same kind of care that the Hebrew-speaking Jewish widows were receiving, the disciples quickly assembled a group of men (the first deacons) to tend to the problem. And in this church with different ethnicities there was a beautiful picture of how the church is to live out this idea of unity in the body. It was a picture of the vision *almost* realized—here on earth. They met from house to house, ate together, and met each other's needs, and God added to the church daily. They embraced the vision. They broke down the walls of resistance to loving those who were different.

This pattern of reconciliation with God and then with our

Christian brothers and sisters was echoed in my life when I came to faith. When I was twenty-seven years old, I was a young husband and father living in Monrovia, California. We had moved to Southern California to escape the racism and segregation that was smothering us in Mississippi. At that time, most of the people in my family were not attending church regularly. My son Spencer, however, had started attending a neighborhood Good News Club, where kids learned about the Bible while playing games and having fun.

I had learned to hate the white people of Mississippi. And if I had not met Jesus I would have died carrying that heavy burden of hate to the grave.

It was connected to a local church. One day, Spencer came home and began to share with me what he had been learning about Jesus. He learned that Jesus was God's Son, who had come to earth to die in our place so we could be forgiven of sins. Before that, I had never heard the good news of God's love in such a clear way. So, when he asked me to go to Sunday school with him at that local church, I agreed.

And in that Sunday school, I finally met Jesus. I discovered that joy is the fulfillment of longing. I was longing for love. I was seeing it in Spencer, but I had never really had it myself. And I heard a verse that sealed the deal: Galatians 2:20. Paul, who had once been a murderer, had been touched by the love of God. He had once hated Christians, but now he was one of them. He explained that the love of God was the reason he was behaving the way he was. He said, "I have been crucified with Christ; and it is no longer I who live, but Christ lives in me; and the life which I now live in the flesh I live by faith in the Son of God, who loved me and gave Himself up for me."

When I heard that verse, I said to myself that if there's a God in heaven who loved me enough to send His only Son into the world to die for me, I want to know that God. I want to *know* Him. And I came to know Him. I believe the purpose of man is to know *that* God, the God of the universe who made everything and holds everything together. That *big* God. That *all-encompassing* God. The God who makes Himself known to humanity. I came to know that God. And I believe the purpose of us knowing that God is to love Him back and make Him known to others.

Almost immediately God began to do something radical in my heart. He began to challenge my prejudices and my hatred toward others. I had learned to hate the white people in Mississippi. I hated their control over our lives. I hated them for what they had done to my brother, Clyde. I hated them for refusing to see me as a person deserving of respect just because I was a human being. I had so much hate! And if I had not met Jesus I would have died carrying that heavy burden of hate to my grave. But He began to strip it away, layer by layer. He reminded me again and again that I could not hoard His love. And I could not be selective about who I would share it with. The love He had shed abroad in my heart was meant to be shared with others regardless of their color.

My good friend Judah Smith says, "You cannot exaggerate God's love. Just try it!" I agree with him. God intends for us to be extravagant and free in our love for one another.

I never imagined when I left Mississippi at the age of sixteen that God would bring me back with a changed heart toward white people. I left Mississippi with hate in my heart. God brought me back with a heart that was overflowing with His love. I had been reconciled to Christ, and He prepared me to return to Mississippi to be reconciled to my white brothers and sisters. Even today when I think back on this, I am overwhelmed at the transforming power of God. God is the ultimate reconciler.

THE CHURCH SHOULD LOOK LIKE THAT

A report in the February 7, 2017, edition of *The Washington Post* grabbed my attention in the best kind of way. It told the story of two churches in Jacksonville, Florida—one black and urban, one white and suburban. They had done what seemed to be impossible. They had merged two years earlier.

Shiloh Metropolitan Baptist Church was a large, 7,000-member black congregation in the heart of the city. It had grown so large that its leaders decided that a second church should be planted in the suburb of Orange Park. At the same time, the mostly white Ridgewood Baptist Church in Orange Park was losing members and was behind on its bills. A Southern Baptist leader who was aware of both churches had an idea. Was it necessary to plant an entirely new church? What if Shiloh and Ridgewood merged into one church with two locations?

Shiloh's charismatic young pastor, H.B. Charles Jr., reflected on the statement made by Dr. Martin Luther King Jr. some fifty years earlier: "Eleven o'clock Sunday morning is the most segregated hour in America." Despite obvious progress over the years, why did that statement still seem as convicting as ever?

"The Bible says that from the church, God is making a tribe

of every nation, people and tongue," Charles told the *Post*. "I feel like the church should look like that."[2] So he did something about it.

Today, Shiloh Metropolitan Baptist looks a lot different than it did in 2014. Located in the city and suburbs, it is now a multiethnic congregation that is made up of both its original Jacksonville congregation and the former Ridgewood Baptist. Some of the Ridgewood families decided not to stick around for the merger, but the congregations moved ahead bravely.

———

It's going to take intentionally multiethnic and multicultural churches to bust through the chaos and confusion of the present moment and redirect our gaze to the revolutionary gospel of reconciliation.

———

More than 250 African American members from the downtown congregation volunteered to move to the suburban location for one year to help grease the wheels of the transition. After twelve months all of them decided to stay at Orange Park. And it wasn't just two churches shuffling the same old folks from one location to the other. What they were doing was so compelling that the community could not help but be drawn to it. A year into the radical experiment, more than a thousand new people joined the church, including several interracial couples who felt they had found a church that understood their unique experiences. And the Orange Park location, which had declined to less than three hundred weekly attenders, was now welcoming more than seven hundred people each Sunday.

Against a backdrop of racial unrest, here was a body of believers courageously living out the message of reconciliation for a divided world to see. This wasn't fake news in *The Washington Post*—it was the good news.

"This is cutting edge," said Ridgewood's senior pastor, Michael Clifford, who became pastor of Christian education for the combined church. "You could take and place [this] in the middle of the Book of Acts and it would make sense, because it is right in the heart and center of what Jesus wants to do."[3]

I've been preaching and teaching on justice and reconciliation for nearly six decades. I've written more than twelve books and spoken to audiences both massive and small. I've experienced firsthand the viciousness of racial hate, but I've also seen the power of God's reconciling love in action. I'm convinced that, more than any speech I've given or book I've written, it's going to take congregations like Shiloh Baptist and Ridgewood in Jacksonville to make the message real. It's going to take intentionally multiethnic and multicultural churches to bust through the chaos and confusion of the present moment and redirect our gaze to the revolutionary gospel of reconciliation.

I really believe that each of our souls yearns for this vision. We want it. We know in our heart of hearts that it is right. As someone once said, "There is a God-shaped vacuum in the heart of each man which cannot be satisfied by any created thing but only by God the Creator, made known through Jesus Christ."[4] I believe that there is a vision-shaped vacuum in the soul of the church that will not be satisfied by man-made strategies or philosophies, but only by His vision of the church victoriously fulfilling the divine mandate.

I'm asking God to help us be captured by this awesome

vision . . . one Church that crosses all ethnic, cultural, class lines. And I pray that He opens our eyes to see that we truly are One Blood, for there is only one race: the human race.

PRAYER · Father God, we praise You for the vision of the church—overflowing with Your character, Your purpose, Your love. Please remove the scales from our eyes and help us to see it, to know it, to embrace it, to love it. Then Lord, overshadow the doubts and fears that so easily war against the vision and help us to be Your Church, overflowing with Your glorious character in this world. By Your awesome power, oh God, make us one that Your Name may be glorified and praised in all the earth!

ONE RACE, ONE BLOOD

"And He made from one man every nation of mankind to live on all the face of the earth, having determined their appointed times and the boundaries of their habitation, that they would seek God, if perhaps they might grope for Him and find Him, though He is not far from each one of us." —ACTS 17:26-27

And they sang a new song, saying, "Worthy are You to take the book and to break its seals; for You were slain, and purchased for God with Your blood men from every tribe and tongue and people and nation." —REVELATION 5:9

I've known that I'm black for as far back as I can remember, so the question of whether race exists was never an issue for me. I knew the color of my skin, and I knew the insanity it triggered in some people. So it would've seemed ridiculous for someone to tell me that race doesn't exist when I saw it in the mirror every day!

At the same time, I had no doubt about my dignity as a person of color. Maybe other folks didn't think I was worth anything, but I knew deep in my heart that I was. When I became a committed Christian at age twenty-seven, I realized that the reason why I always had that sense of self-worth was because God had planted it within me even while I was in my mother's womb. "Your eyes have seen my unformed substance; and in Your book were all written the days that were ordained for me, when as yet there was not one of them" (Ps. 139:16).

But even before reading the book of Psalms, I understood from the Genesis account God's intimate interaction with Adam when He created him, breathing into him the very breath of life. I understood that God was literally breathing dignity and character into this man Adam.

I love how James Weldon Johnson described the creation story:

> Up from the bed of the river
> God scooped the clay;
> And by the bank of the river
> He kneeled him down;
> And there the great God Almighty
> Who lit the sun and fixed it in the sky,
> Who flung the stars to the most far corner of the night,
> Who rounded the earth in the middle of his hand;
> This great God,
> Like a mammy bending over her baby,
> Kneeled down in the dust
> Toiling over a lump of clay
> Till he shaped it in is his own image;
>
> Then into it he blew the breath of life,
> And man became a living soul.[1]

From this one man, Adam, who was created in the very image of God, the entire human race sprang. So I knew in my heart that I had great worth. And then I started to hear normally intelligent people suggest that race, as we know it, really doesn't exist. They said there is only one race—the *human* race—and that man had created the concept of racial categories. At first, I thought it was one of those well-intentioned "nice Christian" things to say, kind of like "I don't see color." But then I began hearing it from other folks—professors, theologians, and scientists. Suddenly, familiar scripture passages took on a different meaning; for example:

- *Then God said, "Let Us make man in Our image, according to Our likeness . . ." (Gen. 1:26)*

- *"Do we not all have one father? Has not one God created us? . . ." (Mal. 2:10)*

- *"And He made from one man every nation of mankind . . ." (Acts 17:26)*

- *. . . there is no distinction between Greek and Jew, circumcised and uncircumcised, barbarian, Scythian, slave and freeman, but Christ is all, and in all. (Col. 3:11)*

None of these disprove the existence of race, but they seemed to point to something greater in God's design for humanity. As I studied the Bible, the threads came together in unexpected ways, and I was forced to pay attention. Did I have the wrong idea about race?

THE MYTH OF "RACE"

In 2000, I wrote the foreword to a book by my friend Dave Unander called *Shattering the Myth of Race: Genetic Realities and Biblical Truths.* The book makes the case that human beings are much more alike than different when it comes to our genetic makeup, and that the term "race" suggests more genetic categories among groups of human beings than is supported by the scientific evidence. The book concludes by looking at the history of how science and the Bible have been abused to justify racism in society. Today Dave (who is white) is a professor of biology at Eastern University outside of Philadelphia, but I first met him in 1976 when he was a college student. Both he and his future wife, Christine, had come to Mendenhall to work with us at Voice of Calvary for the summer. It's been inspiring to see how he has translated his commitment to reconciliation into his life's work as a scholar of genetics, and I'm grateful to have played a part in his development.

Reading Dave's book helped me make sense of some of the troubling questions I was left with regarding race and whether it actually exists. What he talks about in his book drives home the point that race as we know it today is mostly a social theory that was devised and refined over the centuries to serve the economic and religious goals of a majority culture, first in European territory, then later in America. Whiteness, it turns out, is a very recent idea in the grand scheme of history, but it's a powerful one that was used to create categories and systems that would place value, economically and otherwise, on skin color and the groups of people who were either blessed or burdened by it. If race could be used to indicate a group's level of intelligence, its work ethic, and its tendency to do wrong, then the majority culture could justify all types of bigotries and discriminations.

As I read Dave's book, I also was reminded of the famous

"doll experiments" conducted by African American psychologists Kenneth and Mamie Clark in the 1940s. When the Clarks gave African American children choices between black and white dolls, the couple found that more black children preferred the white dolls and attributed more positive traits to dolls of lighter shades. It was a groundbreaking study that exposed how segregated schools were negatively affecting the perceptions of black students and leading to feelings of inferiority and self-hatred. The Clarks' studies helped lead to the US Supreme Court's ruling to desegregate schools, but years later I could still see firsthand how the study's findings about self-hatred played out in the lives of the black youths I worked with. This proved to me that even though race might be a socially manufactured idea, it has had a very real impact on our lives.

Dave warns the church about the "myth of race" and the ways that we've allowed cultural understandings of race to infect our theology and how we view each other. "There is only the human race," he writes, "from every perspective: biological, historical, and in God's Word, the Bible. For the past five hundred years, Western society has been playing out a role in a drama written by the Enemy of our souls, the myth of the master race, and every act has been a tragedy. It's time to change the script."[2]

In addition to allowing God to change our hearts, I'm convinced that changing the script will mean changing the way we read the Bible. At the very least, it will help us be more alert to the ways that cultural prejudices have crept into our understanding of the Bible.

RACE AND THE BIBLE

In the book of Genesis, Adam and Eve are introduced as the first human beings. The Old Testament tells us that humanity started as just one human race.

But throughout Christian history we can find Scripture passages that were misread, mishandled, or misinterpreted for the sake of making the Bible line up with people's cultural biases and agendas. Brandon O'Brien's *Misreading Scripture with Western Eyes* has a section on race that sheds a lot of light on this issue. Race is a fertile target for this kind of wrong thinking. But the Bible talks more about ethnic categories than anything having to do with race. The Greek word *ethnos* (usually translated as "nation") is used in the New Testament to capture the idea of people who make up different groups based on a common history, language, or geographic region.

"Ethnic distinctions are general characteristics that include a person's nation of origin, language, lineage, customs, and outward features, such as skin color," explains my friend Norman Anthony Peart, a trained sociologist as well as the pastor of Grace Bible Fellowship, a multiethnic congregation in Cary, North Carolina. He adds, "When familiar racial identifiers such as skin color are used in the Bible, it is to distinguish and differentiate between people and people groups."[3] He points to the description of Simeon in Acts 13:1 as an example: "Among the prophets and teachers of the church at Antioch of Syria were Barnabas, Simeon (called 'the black man'), Lucius (from Cyrene), Manaen (the childhood companion of King Herod Antipas), and Saul" (NLT).

Norman (who is African American) says these efforts to distinguish between people are a reasonable practice that humans use to discern the differences in the world around them.

It's when we use these practices to generalize or discriminate against others that it becomes a problem, both in secular and religious contexts. "The Bible does not present racial identifiers as indicators of the possession or lack of possession of innate abilities and qualities," Norman says, adding that the only instances where whole people groups are cast negatively in Scripture are when they collectively fail in their obedience to God. It's not about their ethnicity or nationality but their spiritual integrity.

Nevertheless, over the years some church leaders have used stories such as the mark of Cain in Genesis 4:1–17 and the curse of Ham in Genesis 9:20–27 to justify the separation of people based on skin color, as well as their supremacist views. In these wrong, and racially motivated interpretations, God punished Cain for murdering Abel by exiling him to the land of Nod, and later God cursed the offspring of Noah's son Ham, who became the forefather of many African nations. Neither of these readings holds much water. There's nothing in the text, for instance, that describes the physical form of Cain's mark or that suggests it was something passed down through his descendants. In addition, the "mark" itself was not placed on Cain to make him a target for oppression, as some racist scholars have taught, but to make it clear (in God's mercy) that no one else should seek to harm Cain. Likewise, Noah's curse on Ham is not described in detail. In fact, it appears this "curse" was placed on Ham's son Canaan, not Ham or his other sons. Also, the curse seems to be fulfilled when the children of Israel take possession of the land of Canaan (see Josh. 21:43). So, the once-popular idea among some Christians that the black race is inferior and deserving of being enslaved because of a divine curse does not hold up under examination.

The Bible says God made all nations from one blood. This tells me that He intended that humankind would be a people that were spiritually connected despite their cosmetic variations. This speaks directly to the call in 2 Corinthians 5 for people to be reconnected (or reconciled) to both God and their fellow man. This connection is a spiritual one.

We know just from looking at God's creation that He delights in diversity, even as that diversity is rooted in common traits. Did you know, for example, that there are more than 31,000 species of fish? They make up endless varieties of colors, shapes, and behaviors, yet they are all fish. There's a reason why God did it this way. I believe He loves to showcase unity amid diversity.

But the diversity sometimes grows out of God's correction of sin and His need to redirect human attention. In the story of Babel (see Gen. 11:1–9), when we see God scatter the group of folks who had decided to "make a name for themselves" by constructing a state-of-the-art tower to the heavens, He was addressing their pride and rebellion. Apparently, God had plans for them to not just cluster in one spot but to be missional—to spread out to accomplish His purposes. (God's redemptive plan, evidently, was already in motion.) But these people saw greater opportunities for themselves by staying in one place and building a city that would celebrate their own brilliance. Their pride foreshadows Paul's words in Romans 1:21 about those who "even though they knew God, they did not honor Him as God or give thanks, but they became futile in their speculations, and their foolish heart was darkened." God had to shake things up in Babel by confusing the people's common speech in order to shift their attention away from themselves and back onto God's purposes. This gave us a world with different languages, and the spark for cultures and ethnic groups to begin forming.

Soon after this we meet Abraham, the faithful servant whom God would use to reset mankind's priorities and bring the world back into fellowship with Him. When we meet him, Abraham is a fallen person just like everyone else, but he's also a committed believer. Through his faith he would become a "friend of God" (James 2:23). In a time of faithlessness, Abraham believes in God. And his belief becomes the cornerstone of Scripture (see Gen. 12:1–3). He becomes the father of our faith! He becomes the seed through which God will bring people from all nations—of all *ethnos*—back together. God did not promise Abraham that He would make from him a great *race* but a great *nation*. It was God's intention all along to bring forth a nation that could reunite all nations into one.

There is another truth in setting the stories of Babel and Abraham side by side. It is the narrative theme of the spiritual journey. Our natural preference is to stay home, comfortable in our own spirituality. God calls us each on a journey, an Abrahamic journey. It doesn't necessarily mean a geographical journey, but it will always mean a spiritual journey of the heart. It will mean leaving the familiar, traveling in discomfort but being pushed to place our trust in God for . . . everything.

The church in America is at a similar point in history. If we choose to stay in our Babel, our comfortable religion that is man-made and untrue, God will have no choice but to deal with us for our own good, the good of His purposes for the nations and for His own glory. Our only choice is to get on with our Abrahamic journey into the unknown and discomfort of all that it entails. White evangelicalism must choose this transformative journey now. The call is clear. This book is just one of many ways this gospel call is being made. It's time to respond, especially our leadership who should be in tune with God, seizing the moment as they serve as under-shepherds of His people. Some are taking their congregations or their denominations on the journey, and they should be applauded. The majority, however, are camping out in Babel.

HUMANITY WASN'T ALWAYS COLOR-CODED

When I say the human race was not always color-coded, I mean what folks like Dave Unander and Norman Anthony Peart were arguing earlier in this chapter—that race is not a biblical way for us to relate to one another. There's only one race, but over time we've elevated things like skin color, hair texture, language, and ethnicity to a level where they become the main criteria we use to judge entire groups of people. And then we take those classifications and assign them values that we use to include or exclude, to normalize or stereotype, to celebrate or denigrate. We use these things to determine who we hire, the boundaries of neighborhoods, who gets pulled over by police, the length of prison sentences, and on it goes.

This is wrong. This is sin. But sadly, we've let it creep into our churches as well. So, when I say the American church has color-coded Christianity, what I mean is that we've allowed our brokenness around race and class to define how we express our faith and how we value one another. We've put our own cultural preferences and perceptions in place of the radical, upside-down values of God's kingdom. In Matthew 20:16, Jesus says "the last shall be first, and the first last," but we've done everything we can to make sure we're first.

Sometimes I think the American church needs a vision like

the one God sent to Peter in Acts 10. Maybe we need God to tell us in no uncertain terms about our bigotry and our need to show the same grace to others that has been shown to us. We need for Him to challenge us about calling what he has created "common or unclean." Then maybe we can say along with Peter, "I most certainly understand now that God is not one to show partiality, but in every nation the man who fears Him and does what is right is welcome to Him" (Acts 10:34–35).

I'm speaking very broadly, of course. And I include myself in the criticism. We as the American church need to take more ownership for our collective sin, our obsession with things that will not make an ounce of difference in heaven, and our failure (past and present) to stand up and speak up for the poor, for the stranger, for the ones who don't look like us. We need to be awakened to the truth—God's Truth.

America has seen at least three Great Awakenings over the course of our history. With each of them there was a break from complacency and ritual ceremony. God used each of them to inspire movements aimed at healing the ills of society. They were marked by a deep sense of personal conviction and a commitment to a new standard of personal morality. The Second Great Awakening was used by God to stir the hearts of Christians toward the abolition of slavery. The experience of free whites and enslaved blacks worshiping together at these revivals caused many white Christians to begin to question the differences between their spiritual reality and their cultural practice.[4] I'm praying for another Great Awakening where God shakes the Church in America and helps us to see the truth about race and how our misunderstandings have stained the vision.

Race is just one way that we've allowed ourselves to be divided, but it's a big one. And in light of our nation's checkered history with the subject, it's clearly one that we need to do more corporate confession and lamenting about before we can move forward. We'll be talking about that in the next couple of chapters.

That said, I remain optimistic about the future. A recent survey of the National Association of Evangelicals (NAE) indicates that evangelical leaders "unanimously affirmed that reconciliation is a biblical mandate." A majority of those who

---

The next generation of believers is already making it clear that they want to rewrite the script.

---

responded to the survey said that "they have preached, taught or heard a sermon on reconciliation in the last year." The NAE president, Leith Anderson, said, "At the center of the gospel is God's heart to reconcile people to himself and to reconcile people to each other. Racial reconciliation demonstrates the power of the gospel and reflects Christ's work on the cross that brought us near to God."[5]

The Southern Baptist Convention is the largest Baptist denomination in the world. Bruce Gourley describes its origins: "White Baptists in the South withdrew fellowship from their Northern counterparts on May 10, 1845, forming the Southern Baptist Convention in order to better defend the South's practice of, and dependency upon, black slavery."[6] Though they were founded on racial division, they have taken bold steps forward. In 2012 they elected Fred Luter as the first African American president of the denomination. Russell Moore, Ethics and Religious Liberty Commission president, said this at that time: "A descendant of slaves elected to lead a denomination forged to protect the evil interests of slaveholders is a sign of the power of a gospel that crucifies injustice and reconciles brothers and sisters."[7]

They made history again in 2017. For the first time in the denomination's 172-year history, a black pastor, Dr. H.B. Charles Jr., was elected to serve as president of the SBC Pastors' Conference. The Baptist Press reported a statement from Ken Whitten, pastor of Idlewild Baptist Church in Lutz, Florida:

> *"We thought it was time to stop talking about racial unity in positions of leadership within our convention" and "put a president out there . . ." from among the "African Americans, Hispanics and Asians who are pastoring great churches and are very worthy of being in positions of leadership in our convention," said Whitten.*[8]

This move by the Southern Baptist Convention is radical and it is beautiful. It points us to the realization that for reconciliation to be achieved in the church, a place must be made for minorities to serve in positions of leadership. The leadership of the Church must reflect the Revelation 7 vision: "all nations, and kindreds, and people, and tongues" (KJV).

The next generation of believers is already making it clear that they want to rewrite the script. They are eager for change. I've felt their enthusiasm and seen their radical commitment to the Lord. I've encountered the bold and innovative ways that they are stepping forward and bringing their churches along with them!

They are also realists. They've recognized the challenges

of a color-coded Christianity and know that our checkered past requires us to look honestly at our history and lament our mistakes and missteps first. Bono's song "One" reminds us that though we are one, we're different. And we have used our differences to hurt one another again and again. We must go back before we can go forward. Let's go there together. Let's lament our broken past.

PRAYER · Lord God, open our eyes to see Your truth and to believe Your Word. From one man You created all mankind. You made us from one blood. And then You saved us by one blood. The precious blood of Your Son Jesus. Your Word is truth. Help it to penetrate our hearts and our minds. Help it to break through our walls of resistance and those places where we've chosen to believe the Enemy's lies. Break us, Lord. Awaken us, Lord. Make us one.

LIVING IT OUT

Mosaic Church[1]
LEAD PASTOR: Dr. Mark DeYmaz

LITTLE ROCK, ARKANSAS

In the fall of 2000, Precious Williams began cutting my hair. She was close, the cut was cheap, and I particularly enjoyed talking with her about racial attitudes in the southern United States. As an African American who grew up in Central Arkansas, Precious was a valued teacher and person of genuine warmth. Indeed, I not only learned much from her, but that fall, God used Precious to change my life.

I remember sitting in her chair one day and initially enjoying light-hearted conversation. At some point, however, we began talking about racism and, in particular, the segregation of the local church. I asked Precious if churches in Little Rock had always been segregated and what it was like for her growing up in such a place. Had it affected her spiritually? Had it shaped her view of Christians, of the Church of God?

"Precious," I said, "do you think there is a need in Little Rock for a diverse church, one where individuals of varying backgrounds might worship God together as one?"

Her answer was no surprise.

"Oh, yes, Mark," she said, in a quiet but hopeful tone. She went on to describe what she thought such a church might be like—what it would mean for the community—and to say that she longed for the day.

Closing my eyes, I pondered her words. What she said next shook me to my core.

"Mark, do you ever think it could happen here?"

Now when she spoke, I experienced two remarkable things.

Physically, I felt a powerful rush of heat pass through my body— the same terrifying sensation you feel when someone scares you in the dark!

Spiritually, however, something even more remarkable occurred. For though I had heard with my ears—"Mark, do you ever think it could happen here?"—I heard with my heart—"Mark, would you consider doing it here?" Immediately, then, I was transported in my mind to Acts 16 and to a time when God used another individual to issue a similar invitation to a man (the apostle Paul) at a similar crossroads in his life. It was my own Macedonian moment.

Not long after, on May 17, 2001, my wife, Linda, and I responded in prayer to a very specific call of God on our lives. That day, we committed ourselves and our family to a journey of faith, courage, and sacrifice that would lead to the establishment of a multiethnic and economically diverse (nondenominational) church in the heart of Central Arkansas (Little Rock)—a church founded in response to the prayer of Jesus Christ for unity and patterned after the New Testament church at Antioch (Acts 11:19ff.)—a church for others, for all people, a church we called Mosaic.

Who We Are and Why

Mosaic is a multiethnic and economically diverse church founded by men and women seeking to know God and to make Him known through the pursuit of unity, in accordance with the prayer of Jesus Christ (John 17:20–23) and patterned after the New Testament church at Antioch (Acts 11:19–26; 13:1ff.).[2] Mosaic is not, however, a church focused on racial reconciliation. Rather, we are focused on reconciling men and women to God through faith in Jesus. Through these statements, we make clear that our church is focused on two primary works of reconciliation: first, on reconciling men and women to God through faith in Jesus Christ and second, on reconciling a local body of believers with the principles and practices of New Testament churches that existed at Antioch, Ephesus, and Rome.

Stated another way, we believe that when men and women of diverse backgrounds are one with God individually, they can and should walk, work, and worship God together as one collectively, in and through the local church, in order to advance a credible witness of God's love for all people; that is, for the sake of the gospel.

Thus, at Mosaic, we are and remain committed to evangelism, discipleship, community engagement and transformation—simple as that.[3]

This Should Be Our Finest Hour

Never in my lifetime have the people of this country been so at odds with one another. Sure, there've been challenges, obstacles, and disagreements in the past; but they were usually limited to one or two issues at a time. Today, however, no matter where you turn, people are bowed up, choosing sides, and vilifying those who disagree with them on matters of race, class, culture, gender, religion, politics, and even on whether to stand, sit, or kneel during the playing of our national anthem. Thanks to social media, the battles are not only ongoing but also fueled daily by new videos, hashtags, and memes in support of one opinion or another.

Could it be for such a time as this that God has brought us here:

- To a place of passion and understanding?

- To disrupt the status quo?

- To repurpose the church to redeem the community?

Indeed, this should be our finest hour.[4]

By establishing healthy multiethnic and economically diverse churches of Christ-centered faith, we can both learn from and lead others to navigate the rough seas of division. By walking, working, and worshiping God together as one, we can get beyond the distinctions of this world that so often and otherwise divide. In so doing, we "bring to light what is the administration of the mystery which for ages has been hidden in God who created all things; so that the manifold (Gr., *polypoikilos*—"marked with a great variety of colors") wisdom of God might now be made known through the church . . . " (Eph. 3:9–10) In so doing, we can shape the future of things to come.

That said, let us not promote or pursue such a dream because it is politically correct, but because it is biblically correct; not so much because it's nice, but because it's necessary.[5]

Yes, by building healthy multiethnic and economically diverse churches, we can (collectively) get beyond rhetoric to results, beyond words to wins, for the glory of God. By taking intentional steps, empowering diverse leaders, developing cross-cultural relationships, pursuing cross-cultural competence, and promoting a spirit of inclusion, the local church gains credibility. By appealing to more than a single demographic, unity and diversity gives us broader influence in the community. In this way, we pave the path of peace (Matt. 5:9), our light so shines (Matt. 5:16), and Christ is lifted up so as to draw all men and women to Himself (John 12:32).

This is the power of unity. This is the gospel of Christ.

A LAMENT FOR OUR BROKEN PAST

"Blessed are those who mourn, for they shall be comforted."
—MATTHEW 5:4

The concept of lament is heavy. It can seem foreboding and dark if we don't remind ourselves that we're only looking back so that we can move forward with His power. Let me make a bold statement: *There is no institution on earth more equipped and capable of bringing transformation to the cause of reconciliation than the Church.* But we have some hard work to do.

In many ways this is like a marathon. The marathon runner has to make it through the "wall." Some runners describe this wall as sudden fatigue and loss of energy. If the runner can endure and make it through, he can run the rest of the race with a steady pace of endurance, always keeping his eyes on the finish line. He gets energized as he sees the finish line approaching. And he is often overwhelmed with joy and exuberance when he finally finishes the race. In my heart of hearts I want us to be able to make it through the "wall" of lament and see the joy that awaits us at the finish line. We will rejoice together praising Him for the victory. But to get there, we must lament. Let's do it together.

Though it has been eighty-seven years since my mother passed away, I still lament her passing. From deep down in my soul I mourn that she died for reasons that should have been preventable. The doctor's diagnosis was that she died of pellagra. In everyday man's language that means that she literally starved to death. In a country of plenty and excess she died because her body could not sustain itself and provide nourishment for me. And she died because she was a poor black woman in Mississippi. That's a source of great pain for me when I think about it—even these many years later.

Lament comes from deep down in the soul. We need to give voice to our souls. The god of this world has blinded the eyes of Christians and the eyes of the Church, so we can't see the condition of our souls. But we can feel it; we can feel the gnawing in our souls. That's why I love music so much. It's universal—it skips the eyes and the mind, and goes straight to the soul. You feel it. It shakes you. It stirs you. I believe that's why the music of Scripture—the Psalms—connects so well with us. We can feel what David felt when he cried out to God, "Create in me a clean heart, O God; and renew a right spirit within me" (Ps. 51:10 KJV).

I'm just now finding the depths of private worship . . . and singing songs. It's lifting me. Everybody tells me that I can't sing. But I've learned how to study the Word, how to meditate, and how to listen. That's what I think prayer is: listening to God. But lament? I'm just now learning about it. Henri Nouwen's writings are helping me with that. He wrote from a place of brokenness and was transparent about his pain. He said, "The wounds of our individual lives, which seem intolerable when lived alone, become sources of healing when we live them as part of a fellowship of mutual care."[1]

I may not know much about music. But Spencer, my son, sure did. His mother made him take music lessons. He said, "You play 'Amazing Grace' on the black keys, and you play it at the tune of the sound of the groan of the dying slaves." That's something, isn't it? I think that's called the minor keys. They tug at your soul. You can just hear those old slaves singing "I once was lost, but now am found; was blind but now I see."

The groan of the slave was a lament. As he bent to the ground to pick cotton in the blistering heat of the day, he would cry out from the depths of his soul, "Soon I'll be done with the troubles of the world, troubles of the world, troubles of the world. Soon I'll be done with the troubles of the world. Going home to be with my God." His lament was for a world gone evil. It was his cry to the God of heaven who he knew held the balance.

The soul is the ultimate truth teller. It knows truth. And from the very soul of the Church—we need to grieve our refusal to obey His command to love one another. Each person,

---

More than one-third of the Psalms are laments.

---

each individual offers a unique representation of God's image. We need to know each other, love each other, serve alongside each other, and worship with each other to truly know the fullness of who God is. When I remember the vision of Revelation and remember the experience of Pentecost, there's an ache in my soul. We are so far, far away.

More than one-third of the Psalms are laments. They allow

the psalmist to cry out to God in anguish, knowing that He alone is the ultimate healer and justifier. We see lament used often in Scripture as the Old Testament prophets warned Judah and Israel of God's soon coming judgment. When Isaiah wrote concerning the coming judgment on Judah he said, "her gates will lament and mourn, and deserted she will sit on the ground" (Isa. 3:26). One reason Jeremiah is called "the weeping prophet" is because the entire book of Lamentations consists of laments warning of God's judgment and righteous indignation.

But the laments of Scripture do more than just voice painful emotions and serve as an outlet that gives vent to our pain. These psalms of lament stand alone as theology. They teach us about our God and how to worship Him. They transform us.[2]

I agree with Michael Card when he says, "Jesus understood that lament was the only true response of faith to the brokenness and fallenness of the world. It provides the only trustworthy bridge to God across the deep seismic quaking of our lives. . . . It seems to me that we do not need to be taught *how* to lament. What we need is simply the assurance that we *can* lament. We all carry deep within ourselves a pressurized reservoir of tears. It takes only the right key at the right time to unlock them. . . . in God's perfect time, through lament, when these tears are released, they can form a vast healing flood."[3]

Scripture was never intended to be used solely for individual application. It was meant for the community of believers. The psalms of lament were meant to be tools in the community worship experience to bring the worshipers into the presence of our God. The lament is His gift to us, His church. They urge us to come and be healed together.

We see a noticeable pattern to the laments in Scripture:

1. **A desperate cry:** The lament begins with a cry to the Lord. The psalmists came to God with pure, raw emotion. There was no phoniness or need to speak in measured tones or cautiously. Some of their cries almost border on a challenge to God as the One who has abandoned His people. The beauty of our God is that He allows this! He wants us to empty our hearts of this heaviness. I don't know about you but I am desperate for God to move in this area of reconciliation. I know that without his Spirit moving on all of our hearts, nothing will happen for good. Consider Psalm 13:1–2: "How long, O LORD? Will You forget me forever? How long will You hide Your face from me? How long shall I take counsel in my soul, having sorrow in my heart all the day? How long will my enemy be exalted over me?"

2. **A petition/request for help:** The psalmist then appeals to the Lord for help. We've been looking in all of the wrong places for help in fighting this battle for reconciliation. We've sought help from social service agencies and government programs. But this is something that requires divine power.

Often the request in Scripture is to destroy enemies, heal a wound, or whatever their need is—they see God as the One who can fix it. That's David's request in Psalm 13:3–4: "Consider and answer me, O LORD my God; enlighten my eyes, or I will sleep the sleep of death, and my enemy will say, 'I have overcome him,' and my adversaries will rejoice when I am shaken."

3. **A concluding praise:** In spite of the darkness of soul of the lament, the psalmist acknowledges that God is Sovereign,

He is omnipotent, and He is worthy of praise. The lament concludes with exaltation and a commitment to trust in God, regardless of the circumstances. David ends his lament in Psalm 13:5–6 with a powerful proclamation of praise: "But I have trusted in Your lovingkindness; my heart shall rejoice in Your salvation. I will sing to the LORD because He has dealt bountifully with me!"

Hip-hop artist Trip Lee's song "I Don't Know" is based on this psalm. He uses it as a model to help express grief over the death of his friend's son and over racially motivated shootings in our nation. This young hip-hop artist and preacher has discovered that lament connects deeply with his audience. "I want people to contemplate what it looks like to bring our complaints before God—what it looks like to doubt him, but to strive to wrestle with him and see what it looks like to trust him during those hard times."[4]

The Church should rightly grieve for our failure in living into the fullness of God's light. But we have a problem. In our Western world we don't do well with grief and suffering. Our rugged individualism has trumped the call to shared grief. And many of us believe that it shows a lack of faith to lament. We want to move too quickly to our claims of victory in Jesus. We neglect the need within our souls to cry out. It is much easier to ignore the aching in our souls. But I love the church, and my heart's desire is to see her well. My love for the church compels me to cry out and to sound the alarm.

What would this kind of lament look like today? How can the Church come together to grieve our failure and appeal to Him for healing? And what do we have to lament over? I would argue that we have much to lament. But before we get started, let me prepare you for what lies ahead. It can be agonizing to dig up the deep wounds of our history. Like lancing a boil, there is excruciating pain before the final release of the venomous pus. It's hard and painful work. But we can be encouraged by the example of our Christ who endured the agony and suffering of the cross in order to purchase our salvation. "Fixing our eyes on Jesus, the author and perfecter of faith, who for the joy set before Him endured the cross, despising the shame, and has sat down at the right hand of the throne of God" (Heb. 12:2). While there was agony on one side of Calvary, on the other side of Calvary there was a redeemed Church, the bride of Christ. Lament and confession live on the agonizing side of reconciliation, but on the other side there is the church victorious. Let's keep this in mind as we do the hard work of lamenting. We have much to lament . . .

OUR CLAIMS TO SHAME

Divided on Sunday

It was Billy Graham who said it first, and Martin Luther King Jr. echoed it from his jail cell in Birmingham: Sunday at 11:00 a.m. in America is still the most segregated of times. This charge was made against the Church in the 1950s, and sadly it is still true today. As of 2012 only about 20 percent of churchgoers attended ethnically diverse churches, where no one ethnic group makes up more than 80 percent of the congregation.[5] I acknowledge that this is difficult to accomplish if the surrounding neighborhood of the church is homogenous. But if that's not the case, we should be active in pursuing those who don't look like us. God's vision for His Church is one body, unified around the purpose of bringing Him glory so that the watching world would know Him—and would be compelled to follow Him. Our lack of unity has given the world cause to doubt His power and His existence.

It all began in 1787. Richard Allen, a freed slave who had purchased his own freedom joined St. George's Methodist Episcopal Church, in Philadelphia. Blacks and whites worshiped together—but not really *together*. Allen became frustrated with the limitations the church placed on him and the other black parishioners, limitations that included segregating pews. He left the church and founded the African Methodist

------

We enthusiastically fought for the end of segregation in the school system, yet we have not fought at all for the integration of the church.

Episcopal Church (AME), the first independent black denomination in the United States. He focused on organizing a denomination where free blacks could worship without racial oppression and where slaves could find a measure of dignity.

What happened in the Methodist church was repeated across the country and across denominations with the end of slavery. The black church in America came about because segregation was practiced in the North and in the South. We were not welcome in white churches. It is to our shame that since 1787, not nearly enough has changed in the church.

The shame for this practice is a shared shame. While it is true that blacks were not initially welcome in white churches, we have not made significant efforts toward change since that time. We could reasonably say, in the past, that we were respecting the law of the land—but this is no longer true.

We have worn our separateness as a badge of honor and have been content to maintain our separate worship experiences. We enthusiastically fought for the end of segregation in the school system because we understood that separate always meant unequal. Yet we have not fought at all for the integration of the church. We must answer for this unfortunate truth.

Misuse of Scripture

We've already discussed how the mark of Cain and the curse of Ham were used by Christians to defend the institution of slavery and to protect the interests of slave owners. Other verses of Scripture were used as well. Verses like Ephesians 6:5 ("slaves, be obedient to those who are your masters according to the flesh, with fear and trembling") and Titus 2:9 ("urge bondslaves to be subject to their own masters in everything, to be well-pleasing, not argumentative") were used to justify the inhumane treatment of slaves. Even from Old Testament times it was understood that involuntary servitude was not pleasing to God. Consider these verses: "He who kidnaps a man, whether he sells him or he is found in his possession, shall surely be put to death" (Ex. 21:16).

The type of servitude that Scripture endorsed was indentured service. In those cases the bondservant willingly chose to work for his master for a determined amount of time. At the end of that time he was free. Any slave who ran away from his master (thus expressing his desire for freedom) was to be welcomed by the Israelites, not mistreated, and not returned. Deuteronomy 23:15–16 says: "You shall not hand over to his master a slave who has escaped from his master to you. He shall live with you in your midst, in the place which he shall choose in one of your towns where it pleases him; you shall not mistreat him."

Scripture tells us of an escaped slave whose name was

Onesimus. He had run away from his master, Philemon. Onesimus met Paul while he was in prison in Rome or Caesarea and became a believer. What Paul asked him to do after giving his life to Christ was radical. He insisted that Onesimus return to his master. And he appealed to Philemon to accept Onesimus not as a slave, but now as a brother in Christ. Both Philemon and Onesimus were now sons of Paul's ministry and he desired for them to each recognize the other as brothers.

The message is a powerful one. It signals the truth that even if there are differences in how people are viewed in the culture, it must not be so within the church. Within the church there are to be no second-class citizens. No stepchildren.

Missed Kingdom Opportunity

Tony Evans (pastor of Oak Cliff Bible Fellowship, Dallas, Texas, and the first African American to graduate from Dallas Theological Seminary) argues in his book *Oneness Embraced* that God allowed slavery for two reasons. The first was so that the slaves' concept of God would be fully complete. Coming from Africa they had a robust, rich knowledge of God as Father; yet they did not have a full and complete knowledge of God the Son.[6] The slave did come to know Jesus Christ the Son of God in fulfillment of this initial purpose, and their coming to faith presented a challenge to the church in this country. Would they throw their doors open and welcome these new brothers and sisters, or would they treat these black family members as second-class citizens?

According to Dr. Evans, the second aim that God intended addresses this question. God's intent was for the white slave owner to learn and practice biblical love. Slavery provided a day-to-day opportunity for the white slave owner to demonstrate love and compassion. It offered an opportunity for him to see the image of God in the face of the slave and to acknowledge and affirm the dignity of the individual. This would have been a powerful witness to the power of God if it had happened. Unfortunately, for the most part, this aim was not fulfilled at all. Instead, the devil's lie of two different races prevailed. When you live a lie it destroys everyone involved. For the slave master, his conscience was seared as the love of money, and economic gain overruled his concern for his fellow man. And for the slave, his sense of dignity and personhood was assaulted without recourse.

Shortsighted Vision

God intended that together, blacks and whites in one church would be that city on a hill. We would light the way for those in darkness. We would urge the hurting masses to come meet a Savior who could fill the longing in their hearts. We would do this by reaching out to the poor and acting on behalf of those who are marginalized in our country. We would understand that social justice is not an added-on aspect for the church or for believers, but that it is part of our gospel imperative. It is part of the gospel of reconciliation—the gospel of one blood. We would know this because we are people of the Word.

Throughout the Old Testament the people of God were commanded to care for the stranger and for the poor. Jeremiah 22:3 says, "Thus says the LORD, Do justice and righteousness, and deliver the one who has been robbed from the power of his oppressor. Also do not mistreat or do violence to the stranger, the orphan, or the widow; and do not shed innocent blood in this place." And in Isaiah 1:17, "learn to do good; seek justice, reprove the ruthless, defend the orphan, plead for the widow."

Jesus offered a strong challenge to His followers and to us

in the New Testament: "Then He will also say to those on His left, 'Depart from Me, accursed ones, into the eternal fire which has been prepared for the devil and his angels; for I was hungry, and you gave Me nothing to eat; I was thirsty, and you gave Me nothing to drink; I was a stranger, and you did not invite Me in; naked, and you did not clothe Me; sick, and in prison, and you did not visit Me.'

"Then they themselves also will answer, 'Lord, when did we see You hungry, or thirsty, or a stranger, or naked, or sick, or in prison, and did not take care of You?' Then He will answer them, saying, 'Truly, I say to you, to the extent that you did not do it to one of the least of these, you did not do it to Me.' These will go away into eternal punishment, but the righteous into eternal life" (Matt. 25:41–46).

We have chosen to ignore this huge aspect of biblical reconciliation to our own harm.

"We are inevitably our brother's keeper because we are our brother's brother."
MARTIN LUTHER KING JR.

Misdirected Missions

Throughout the history of the church in America, our missions efforts have been focused on developing continents and countries: Africa, Asia, South America, Haiti . . . while the ethnic neighborhoods in our own country were ignored. Some well-meaning Christians have a theology of mission that seeks to heal the spiritual and physical suffering of people far away, but pays little attention to needs here at home.

My friend Brian Fikkert writes about this imbalanced approach to missions in *When Helping Hurts*. He observes that short-term missions have become a $1.6 billion annual enterprise in America.[7] Every year, thousands of Christians spend anywhere from $1,000 to $3,000 per person to go across the globe to take the gospel to the world—all the while ignoring the gaping wound in the communities near home.[8]

Martin Luther King Jr. once said, "All of life is interrelated. . . . We are inevitably our brother's keeper because we are our brother's brother. Whatever affects one directly affects all indirectly."[9]

Lack of Remorse

Perhaps the strongest indictment against us as the Church is that we have settled for an Americanized version of the Church that mirrors whatever culture says, and there is no collective sense of loss, no sense of remorse. We have sinned deeply. The problem is that we haven't got a taste of the sinfulness of racism. We don't see the wickedness of color-coding. We don't see the wickedness of profiling God's people that He

---

Possibly the closest we have come to national lament in recent times was immediately after September 11, 2001.

---

has created to be one and that He has created in His image. And we are piecemealing it. What we are doing is too little, too late. The problem is that society is being lied to. Racism is based on a lie. God created one race, one blood. That's the human race. The very idea of the gospel is that we would be one. The world would know that we are Christians because of our oneness, and because of our love.

Jesus intentionally brought together disciples who were very different—fishermen, tax collectors—not people who would naturally love one another. But he did this to show us what love looks like in practice. We have the privilege of putting this same kind of love on display as we love those in the body of Christ who don't look like us.

It troubles me that there is no outrage at our collective failure to rise up to God's call to oneness. In the Old Testament when Ezra returned to Jerusalem with the exiles and discovered that they had violated God's law by intermarrying with foreign wives, the people of Israel gathered for a time of corporate lament.

"Now while Ezra was praying and making confession, weeping and prostrating himself before the house of God, a very large assembly, men, women and children—gathered to him from Israel, for the people wept bitterly" (Ezra 10:1). And then in verse 6: "Then Ezra rose from before the house of God and went into the chamber of Jehohanan the son of Eliashib. Although he went there, he did not eat bread nor drink water, for he was mourning over the unfaithfulness of the exiles."

Possibly the closest we have come to national lament in recent times was immediately after September 11, 2001. For a few days business as usual ceased. Americans shared a feeling of collective shock and a sense of deep mourning over the lives that were lost and the alarming state of our world. Church doors were kept open throughout the day, welcoming people in to find comfort. Years ago Americans experienced periods of national lament with the assassinations of President John F. Kennedy, Bobby Kennedy, and Martin Luther

King Jr. With each of these instances there was a recognition that something horrific had happened—lives had been taken away mercilessly—and such tragic events called for a time of mourning, reflection, and assessing what had happened. Our nation united around a deep, abiding concern and effort to make sure such a thing never happened again.

For the church, corporate lament requires that we acknowledge that something horrific has happened. Something that greatly grieves the heart of our God has happened in His church. We have abandoned His call to oneness and terribly missed the mark Christ set in John 17. May God remove the scales from our hardened hearts and help us to see with eyes of truth.

My Lament

Oh God! What do we do when the foundations are shaken!
There's hate, distrust, and selfish greed in Your Church
We're doing the wrong things with wrong motives . . .
We're not one and we are satisfied.

Lord, open our eyes to see Your Truth
Awaken in us a zeal for Your power and Your presence
among us
Break down the walls that have separated us
Help us to love with Your love

From the earliest of our existence You, O Lord, have kept us
Your Word has been a lamp and a light for our path
For all of our appointed days we will serve You
From everlasting to everlasting—You are our God.

In the summer of 2018, the Equal Justice Initiative will unveil a memorial that will consist of large tablets hanging from a square structure placed on a hill overlooking downtown Montgomery, Alabama. The tablets will serve as visual reminders of more than 800 counties where lynchings took place in this country. They will be engraved with the names of those lynching victims. The hope is that this memorial will become a place of mourning and remembrance, a place to lament and possibly even to corporately confess. These are the kinds of things that must happen if we are ever going to deal with the corporate sins of our past history.[10]

Lament can be powerful. But it falls short of the goal of biblical reconciliation if it doesn't also encourage confession. Confession draws the issue closer to home and helps each of us to account for individual responsibility. Let's go there next.

PRAYER · Lord God, grant that we may see and know the measure of Your displeasure with us as we claim to belong to You yet choose to be separate from one another. May the fire of Your Spirit burn within our hearts so that we are thrown from our places of complacency and comfort and find ourselves hastening to make You known among the people of the earth, because we Your Church are one.

THE HEALING BALM OF CONFESSION

"And the son said to him, 'Father, I have sinned against heaven and in your sight. I am no longer worthy to be called your son.'"
—LUKE 15:21

I love the story of the prodigal son. I believe that it can teach us much about what we can do to make our way home on this issue of unity in the Church. Most of us, I am sure, are familiar with this parable of a son who was itching to get his inheritance and get out from under the strict rules in his father's home. When this wayward son demanded his inheritance from his father and walked away from his home and his responsibilities, he rejected the standards that his father had set for him. He set his own standard for what was right and good and wasted his resources on selfish living. He learned soon enough that the Enemy had fooled him and all that glittered was not gold. And finally when all of his wealth and possessions were gone he came to himself and realized that the path he was travelling was wrong; it was self-destructive.

In many ways we can say this of the church. We walked

away from the standard that our Father set for the church, and yes, we have wasted our resources on selfish endeavors. We have set many standards for what is right and good. Our standards are often bigger buildings, more people in the pews, more programs, and more money in our capital budgets. And the record is that the church in America is dying. According to The American Church Research Project, "between 1990 and 2009 more than 56 million people were added to the US census (56,819,471);" however, "during the same 20-year span only 446,540 people became active members of a local church; less than 1%."[1] By anyone's standards, that's a church in decline.

THE BEAUTY OF BROKENNESS

There is something so compelling about this prodigal son's confession. And I think what makes it so heartwarming is the humility he demonstrates. It's beautiful because it's such a picture of brokenness. Brokenness is the opposite of pride. It is the willingness to admit our faults without concern for our reputation. It is the willingness to lay down our own rights and do whatever benefits the other. It is putting the needs of the other above our own. It lays the groundwork for reconciliation to occur.

This prodigal son acknowledged that as he sinned against his earthly father, he was also sinning against the God of heaven. Our sins against our brothers and sisters are ultimately against our Father in heaven. As we struggle to become reconciled to one another, this is an essential part of the process. Each of us must "come to ourselves" and own our part in this mess . . . and we must become broken about it. Before the Lord opened my eyes to the call of reconciliation, my part was anger. I wanted to get even. I was tired of being taken advantage of and not being able to fight back. And I was so fearful. My fear and anger were barriers that kept me from reaching out.

The book of Acts shows us another beautiful picture of brokenness. In Acts 16:25–34, we read that Paul and Silas have been imprisoned for preaching the gospel, and at midnight they prayed. God sent an earthquake to shake the very foundations of the prison. Thinking that the prisoners had escaped, the Roman jailer prepared to take his own life. But Paul stopped him and affirmed that none had escaped. At this moment something incredible happens. The Roman jailer was transformed from enemy and abuser to broken and tender healer, as he is confronted with his wrong and the power that is at work within Paul and Silas. He falls trembling before them and asks, "Sirs, what must I do to be saved?" That question is pregnant with power. The strong willingly becomes weak. The superior willingly becomes inferior. *I realize that I have been wrong; that I have wronged you. How can I make it right?* He comes to himself and claims Jesus as Savior, and we see him washing the wounds that perhaps he himself had inflicted. That's powerful!

After the beating I suffered in Brandon, Mississippi, I spent a good deal of time in the hospital. I was broken in body and broken in spirit. I had come to understand that my reaction of anger, hate, and bitterness was as bad as the action of the white jail guards who had beaten me. It was at that point that I was able to see my own brokenness. God used the black and white nurses and doctors at that hospital to wash my wounds. For me they were symbolic of the people who had beaten me. What they did healed more than just my broken body. It healed my heart. I wanted to hate all white people after what happened to me. But God used their compassion and care to break the wall of anger, distrust, and bitterness. He used their kindness to convict me of how wrong I was to harbor bitterness in my heart. He set me free to love them in return.

It may not be "American" to humble ourselves and admit our faults before one another, but if we want to be like Christ this is what we must do.

Oh, how beautiful it would be if we could wash one another's wounds from the evil of racism in the church! That could be the balm that heals us . . . that sets us free . . . that rekindles the light that has long been hidden under a bushel. But those wounds cannot and will not be healed without first being exposed. We must do as the prodigal did and acknowledge that we have sinned against God and against one another.

I spoke at a multicultural church in Seattle not long ago. As I shared my testimony, many of those attending shared their own stories. Many had stories of being dehumanized as a minority. Some told stories of internment of their family and friends. I realized that I might have been guilty at some time of dehumanizing others. I had to repent and ask God for forgiveness. When we do that He promises to forgive us, to remove our sin as far as the east is from the west (Ps. 103:12) But the wounds often remain. Often they leave scabs that have to be gingerly removed . . . until all that is left is a scar. The memory of the hurt.

I know that confession and brokenness are almost un-American terms. We pride ourselves on our rugged individualism and our right to be right. So it may not be "American" to admit our faults and humble ourselves before one another, but if we want to be like Christ this is what we must do. He was equal with God, but He humbled Himself and dwelt among His creation. He got hungry and thirsty just as we do. And He submitted Himself to ridicule and scorn in order to purchase our salvation. He is our example.

"Remember the word that I said to you: 'A slave is not greater than his master.' If they persecuted Me, they will also persecute you. If they kept My word, they will keep yours also" (John 15:20). If Jesus is truly our master, then humility and brokenness will become doable. So, let's do the hard business of confession. Let's do it together.

ANGER AND COMPLACENCY

For many of us black folks, there has been an anger that has not always been managed well. We expected and hoped that one day the playing field would be leveled and we would finally realize the hope that Martin Luther King Jr. spoke of—that day when we would not be judged by the color of our skin but by the content of our character. But that day has not come. In spite of having had a black president and seeing blacks achieve success in virtually every arena of life in America—racism still haunts us.

***

"No matter how famous you are . . . being black in America is tough."

LEBRON JAMES

***

In response to racist graffiti being drawn on his house in Los Angeles recently, LeBron James, famed basketball player, said, "No matter how much money you have, no matter how famous you are, no matter how many people admire you, you know being black in America is tough. And we got a long way to go, for us as a society and for us as African-Americans, until we feel equal in America." He goes on to say, "Hate in America, especially for African-Americans, is living every day, and even though it's concealed most of the time . . . it's alive every single day."[2]

This has always been the reality for our people in this country. And it has sparked a level of anger that we have had to work hard to channel properly. In the years after slavery that energy was channeled to build our own institutions—black colleges, black hospitals, black churches. If we were not welcome in their churches, colleges, hospitals—we would build our own. During the Civil Rights movement, that anger was channeled into nonviolent resistance. We learned from Dr. King's principles of nonviolence, and great advances were won. Those principles taught us that nonviolence accepts suffering without retaliation. We learned that unearned suffering has tremendous power to educate and redeem.

The church was the vehicle that God used to press toward equal rights. We had the high moral ground because we chose to love our enemies and not strike back. We chose the way of love. But we've lost that moral high ground. We have lost control of the anger that in previous generations had fueled our upward movement. We have turned that anger on ourselves, and our cities and communities have become unsafe places. The city of Chicago has become infamous for the numbers of gang shootings on an almost daily basis. But not just Chicago—many other major cities across America have been overtaken with violence.

That we have given up our control of this issue is evident in the fact that the Black Lives Matter movement began outside of the church. We should have sounded the alarm when Michael Brown (Ferguson, Missouri), Eric Garner (Staten Island, New York), and so many others were killed. We should have been leading the marches and speaking truth to power. But instead, too much of our energy and drive has been misdirected toward materialism, comfort, and convenience. Many of us no longer keep our church buildings open to provide a safe harbor for our children after school. We are concerned that our buildings may be torn up. We have shut out the children in our communities who need the influence of God's people and God's Word on their lives. We have become inwardly focused and are not the healing agents we once were. This is part of our confession and we must be broken about it.

PRIDE AND PRIVILEGE

We must also be careful about falling into one of two camps: pride and entitlement. After my beating in Brandon I wanted to be a victim. I can remember that. I wanted to say *I got something to whip them with.* For persons who see themselves as victims it is easy to be ensnared by pride. We can carry our pain as a badge of honor and try to whip others with it. I have tried to be very careful since that incident in Brandon to not use what happened to make me think I was better than my oppressor. I seldom talk about the details of that beating because I don't want to use it in a prideful way to punish whites. This pride can easily slide into a feeling of entitlement. That I'm owed something. To be sure, we are owed respect and honor as a human being. But we must not assume upon this expectation by suggesting that others should do for us what we can do for ourselves.

My friend John Piper (pastor of Bethlehem Baptist Church, Minneapolis) and I contributed a chapter in *Letters to a Birmingham Jail*. His was titled, "Waiting for and Hastening the Day of Multiethnic Beauty." In that chapter he shares his confession about racism. He talks about living "across the highway from a Christian university where interracial dating was forbidden until 2000," and "attending an all-white Baptist

---

Many of my white brothers and sisters may need to confess denying that racism exists.

---

church on Wade Hampton Boulevard which passed a resolution in the early sixties that blacks would not be allowed to attend." He later says, "Before there was AIDS to be afraid of, there was blackness. You might get some of it on you.... I never saw one equal provision for blacks. And not only was it not equal, it was not respectful, it was not just, and it was not loving; therefore, it was not Christian."[3]

He speaks of not knowing a single black person, except for Lucy, their maid. "And my relationship with Lucy taught me, in a surprising way, that it is possible to like someone, and even feel deep affection for someone and treat her graciously, while considering her inferior and as someone to be kept at a distance. This in turn has taught me that those who defend the noble spirit of some Southern slaveholders by pointing to how nice they were to their slaves seem to be naive about what makes a relationship degrading. I also cried when my dog got run over."[4]

Many of my white brothers and sisters may need to confess denying that racism exists, choosing to ignore the implications of privilege, and at times acting to reinforce a double standard. Much has been said about white privilege, and admittedly it can be difficult to address without offending. Let me describe it in this fashion: Through no fault or responsibility of our own, most of us were born in the United States of America. Though poverty does exist in America it exists at a level far above the level of poverty in a Third World country. This could be termed "American privilege." We are afforded certain advantages just because we live in America. It's not something that we should feel guilty about, but it is important for us to be aware of these realities. Especially when we talk with people from some of those Third World countries who have a completely different frame of reference for poverty. In a similar way being white in this country affords certain advantages that can be easily overlooked. Peggy McIntosh, a professor at Wellesley College, shares some of those advantages:

- If I should need to move, I can be pretty sure of renting or purchasing housing in an area that I can afford and in which I would want to live.

- I can be pretty sure that my neighbors in such a location will be neutral or pleasant to me.

- Whether I use checks, credit cards, or cash, I can count on my skin color not to work against the appearance of financial reliability.

- I can do well in a challenging situation without being called a credit to my race.

- I am never asked to speak for all the people of my racial group.

- If a traffic cop pulls me over, I can be sure I haven't been singled out because of my race.[5]

These are just a few of the unseen advantages of being a part of the majority culture in this country. *Time* magazine's newsfeed featured a story in 2015 about a study, "Racism is Real," that showed a white man and a black man both going to apply for a job, buy a car, and buy a house. The black man doesn't get an interview while the white man does; he is charged more for his car; and he is not shown a house that a realtor happily shows the white man. These advantages are very real. And it's frustrating when those who benefit from these advantages deny this reality.[6]

Every black parent has the "talk" with their children when they get ready to start driving. They tell them that if a police officer pulls them over they are to say, Yes, sir or Yes, ma'am. They are to keep their hands in the open and not make any quick movements. This wisdom could literally save their lives. I was pulled over by a policeman when my wife and children were in the car. He said something that paralyzed me. As I sat there afraid to speak, he said, "Do the cat have your tongue?" He wanted to humiliate me and destroy my manhood in front of my children. He wanted me to resist so he could shoot me. A white man getting pulled over doesn't have to think about getting killed. But it's our reality. And each of these kinds of encounters wounds the soul.

The issue of white flight is another topic that is painful to consider. Across the country, from one city to the next, as neighborhoods began to change, the white church and individuals have been too quick to abandon those neighborhoods and escape to suburbia . . . away from the rich mission fields of the city. This should not be so.

I visited the National Museum of African American History and Culture in Washington, D.C. recently and was struck again by the devastating impact of racism in this country. I saw the massive slave ships that were used to deliver men and women from the coasts of Africa to this country. Over the course of the entire slave trade to the New World, according to the Trans-Atlantic Slave Trade Database, 12.5 *million* Africans were shipped to the New World. An incredible 10.7 million survived the dreaded Middle Passage, disembarking in North America, the Caribbean, and South America.[7] They were to be the workforce that would drive the economy of America.

A new American system of slavery would be devised for these slaves, replacing the process of indentured servitude that existed before. Race would be interjected to identify the black slave as the "other." Then their "race" was demonized and placed in a subhuman category. If they were viewed more like animals than human beings, then they could be used as free labor that would enrich their slave masters. They would be used to provide the free labor work force that America was built on. Much of the wealth in this country was built on the backs of the slave system. Many of my white brothers and sisters are beneficiaries of a system that has given them great advantages, while at the same time denying those advantages to others. It's important that this is acknowledged and confessed.

CONFESSIONS WE SHOULD ALL MAKE

And then there are mutual confessions that we should all make. We can all confess that we have done a disservice to our

Lord by creating Him in our own image. Pastor Efrem Smith, in an article in *Outreach Magazine*, says the following:

> *The Son of God, Alpha and Omega, was multiethnic, multicultural. In the family tree of Jesus were the indigenous inhabitants of Israel, Palestine, Ethiopia, Egypt, the Sudan, Libya. If that is true, we need to present it, remember it. Then we need to ask what it means for us, through the Holy Spirit, for that Christ to live in us. We must wrestle with what it means to follow that Jesus, to surrender to that Jesus, to represent that Jesus. He walked our earth as a multiethnic, multicultural, Jewish human being. But we have reduced him from that. In our culture, we have made Jesus look like whoever we are instead of who he is. We have made him white. Western. European. Democrat. Republican. Urban. Handsome. Comfortable.*[8]

And finally, we can all confess to being consumed with fear around this issue. True success in the area of reconciliation will require the mastery of our fears. This fear has people saying, "I can't do it" before they even try. Whites are afraid to cross the divide because they might have to give up some of their power and status. Blacks are afraid because it's a lot of hard work, usually with nothing to show for it at the end of the day. Many of us who have tried to make the effort have found out, like LeBron James, that we're still seen as "the lesser other." But God's Word speaks into our fears: "There is no fear in love. But perfect love casts out fear, because fear involves punishment, and the one who fears is not perfected in love" (1 John 4:18). So the antidote to our fear is His love. It is His love empowering us to extend our hands and hearts to one another.

Believers in the first-century church who were burdened with fear were challenged by the apostle Peter to be willing to endure suffering. "In this you greatly rejoice, even though now for a little while, if necessary, you have been distressed by various trials, so that the proof of your faith, being more precious than gold which is perishable, even though tested by fire, may be found to result in praise and glory and honor at the revelation of Jesus Christ" (1 Peter 1:6–7). Rather than shrinking back and allowing their fears to overwhelm them, these believers that Peter spoke to were encouraged and empowered by this challenge. They refused to deny Christ knowing that their refusal would mean certain death. For many of them this "trial by fire" meant being tied to a stake, covered with tar, and set on fire to light the Roman coliseum as part of Nero's madness.

Those who marched for equal rights in the 60s, both blacks and whites, were willing to risk their lives to end the scourge of segregation and Jim Crow in our country. They risked imprisonment, lynchings, beatings, and much more. May we have the same determination to risk life and limb for the worthy cause of bringing the kingdom of heaven to earth—that we might be one.

Confession is not only good for us as individuals and as churches, it's also healing when denominations speak into this discussion. We spoke earlier about the Southern Baptist Convention's movement on this issue. The Christian Reformed Church, the Wesleyan Church, the Pentecostal Church, and many other denominations have made bold declarations about reconciliation in recent years. In 2016 the Presbyterian Church of America (PCA) confessed that, though their denomination wasn't founded until nine years after the 1964 Civil Rights Act, many of their founding denominational leaders and churches actively worked against reconciliation. "Those churches segregated worshipers by race, barred blacks from membership and black churches from joining presbyteries, participated in and defended white supremacist organizations, and taught that the Bible sanctioned segregation and opposed inter-racial marriage." They also confessed to failing to "lovingly confront our brothers and sisters concerning racial sins and personal bigotry."[9]

They say that confession is good for the soul. I believe this to be true. I believe that it is good for us as individuals—and that it is good for the soul of the Church. But it's not just good—it's essential. It is essential if we are to be reconciled one with another. It opens the door for the healing balm of forgiveness to wash over us. Let's go there next. Let's go there together.

PRAYER · Lord God, help us to love you enough to humble ourselves before one another, confessing those things that we have said and done that have damaged our brothers and sisters. Help us to conquer the fears that have paralyzed us for generations; help us to wash one another's wounds and become the healing community that you died for.

LIVING IT OUT

Fellowship Church
LEAD PASTOR: Albert Tate

MONROVIA, CALIFORNIA

Five years ago, we planted Fellowship Monrovia with the aim of being a gospel-centered, nondenominational, multiethnic, intergenerational church. As lead pastor I had always dreamt of a church that would be a multigenerational congregation composed of whites, blacks, Asian Americans, Latinos, and Native Americans in Monrovia, California. When I dream of the church of Jesus Christ, I think of Revelation 7:9, where people from every nation, tribe, people and language stand before the throne. In the book of Ephesians, the apostle Paul describes the church as God's greatest glory. If we are going to transform the world, we are going to do it through the church. So, on January 15, 2012, one day before the Martin Luther King Jr. holiday, over six hundred people of various races and ethnicities, social classes and political affiliation gathered to worship the Lord.

About a year after we started the church, we established life groups. On the surface, the life groups were not unlike the traditional small groups that many churches form, but beneath the surface we formed small groups that were multigenerational and multicultural. We envisioned members meeting in informal settings and getting to know each other by doing life together. However, the goal was not just to worship together, eat together, or do life together, it was to set the table for a deeper and more profound understanding of true reconciliation.

We knew that as people from different ethnicities formed friendships the issue of race would inevitably come up. Therefore, we began to plan and think about ways that we could facilitate those conversations under the banner of the gospel. We started to ask ourselves what would it look like if we created a Center for Reconciliation. As we continued to pray and ponder how to best launch such a center we landed on the idea that it would be three-tiered. The first tier was a time of lament (mourning and prayer) about the widening racial divides in our country. The second tier involved bimonthly daylong workshops that focused on creating a common vocabulary and strategies that would inform and empower participants to have difficult and emotional conversations, not only with fellow church members but also with their families and communities. The third tier focused on developing lay leaders who would lead members in continuing the conversation. The vehicle for developing lay leaders was taking members on civil rights tours and forming yearlong cohorts that focused on a biblical and historical understanding of reconciliation.

In the winter of 2015, we hosted our first daylong workshop with our entire pastoral team and staff. We knew that if we were going to launch a center for racial reconciliation that we had to "practice what we preached"! We were challenged and encouraged by the candid conversations that took place during and after the workshop. Incidentally, every new intern, pastor, and staff member is required to attend the daylong workshop, and as a consequence our staff is continually engaged in this conversation.

At the end of each workshop, participants provided written evaluations of the workshop. The evaluations were used as a tool for refining the workshop content to be more impactful. For example, because the term "white privilege" is an emotionally loaded concept we had to clarify what it is and what it is not. As a result, our participants were able to have more truthful conversations about race and reconciliation.

Additionally, we learned that there were many powerful pieces of the workshop that acted as a catalyst for change. The workshop allowed people of different races and ethnicities to really hear how race and racism impacted them personally and as a people group. It was common to hear people from all sides painfully express how racism distanced them from the *Imago Dei*. In short, we get to sit with people in their hurt, their pain, and even their lack of understanding.

Practically, our goal is to disciple our body to be proactive and not reactive. For three days last summer, many of us watched as television and computer screens showed violence between police and civilians. Alton Sterling and Philando Castile were shot and killed by police. Then a gunman killed five police officers in Dallas. That week made clear just how much these videos of police violence have become part of our lives.

Because our pastoral team and staff had already been in the conversation, we were able to lead our church and the community in a night of lament. We did not have to worry about the "message" the evening would send—people were in grief and we were prepared. The culmination of that evening ended with the testimony of a retired African-American female police officer who has two adult sons. She tearfully expressed the tension she feels every time her sons travel at night, but also understands the difficult job officers have and the danger they face every day. After she spoke, a white police officer came up to the stage and prayed for her and her sons. It was a beautiful display of the potential and power of reconciliation.

Another example of the power of having difficult conversations was prior to the November 2016 presidential election. Our church had already had a daylong workshop scheduled to provide tools to our congregation on how to move forward regardless of the election results. At the beginning of the workshop, the facilitators reminded the participants that the purpose of the workshop was not to "debrief" the election but to provide useful tools to continue the conversation of race and reconciliation.

At Fellowship Monrovia we believe that we should "just be now who we will be in the end." The apostle John, in Revelation 7:9–10, talks about the throne of God and he gives us a picture of what the end will look like. It's a picture of heaven where every tribe, every tongue and every language is gathered around the throne of God, worshiping and singing, "salvation belongs to our God, who sits on the throne and to the Lamb" (NIV). Every tribe. Every tongue. Every language.

If the picture at the end of the story is a picture of every person imaginable, all in the same place, worshiping God, shouldn't that be what the church looks like today? When we get to heaven, there will not be a white section, a black section, a Latino section, an Asian section and a Native American section. No, there is no homogenization in heaven. There is no separation. What we see is something different: reconciliation. We see a reconciling gospel that does not just reconcile us to God, but it also tears down the dividing wall of hostility between us. It reconciles us to one another.

FORGIVENESS: IT'S IN OUR DNA

"For if you forgive others for their transgressions, your heavenly Father will also forgive you. But if you do not forgive others, then your Father will not forgive your transgressions." —MATTHEW 6:14-15

Forgiveness is the linchpin of reconciliation. It is the soil in which reconciliation takes root and grows. Forgiveness shines the brightest against the stark contrast of the darkest of tragedies. We have seen this truth at work in recent history.

We were all stunned to hear the news. The details of the event were shocking. Dylann Roof, a young white supremacist, wandered into the Emanuel African Methodist Episcopal Church in downtown Charleston, South Carolina, during a Wednesday night Bible study. It was July 25, 2015. When Roof arrived at the church, Bible study was already underway. He sat next to the pastor and listened, only speaking up to disagree when they began to discuss Scripture. When they bowed their heads to pray he stood up and began shooting and screaming racial epithets. At the end, nine were dead and three injured.

At Dylann Roof's bond hearing two days later, the relatives of the victims stood to address him. "I forgive you." "I forgive you." "I forgive you." These three words were spoken again and again as the family members of the Charleston church victims spoke to the accused. It was clear that they were struggling with deep emotion and grief. Yet they chose to forgive rather than to hate . . . many of them saying that they were praying for his soul. The nation watched, spellbound.

A lawyer for one of the families said this: "That's genuinely who these people are. That's in their DNA. And for those of us who do not have that same faith, it's hard to imagine—but it's ingrained in them."[1]

Forgiveness is made possible by the power of the Holy Spirit. But that does not mean it is easy.

The attack was intended to provoke a race war in the heart of the old Confederacy. But instead of war, Charleston erupted in grace following the examples of these people of faith. "Blacks and whites filled the miles-long Ravenel Bridge in a show of unity, and within days the most contentious public symbol of South Carolina's Civil War past, the Confederate battle flag, was removed from the state capitol grounds with relatively little of the controversy that had surrounded it for decades."[2]

Forgiveness was on display nine years earlier in Lancaster County, Pennsylvania. On October 2, 2006, Charles Carl Roberts IV walked into an Amish schoolhouse carrying a weapon. After demanding that the adults and boys leave, he told the girls to lie down on the floor facing the chalkboard. He tied their hands and feet and told them that they would have to suffer because God had taken the life of his infant daughter only twenty hours after she was born. He then began to shoot. When it was over ten little girls, ages six to thirteen, had been shot. Five of them survived.

The national media rushed to the scene to report all of the sad, horrific details. They were stunned to discover that there would be no press conferences where the family members would rail against gun violence. No anger-filled speeches condemning the killer. They would see these Amish "gentle people" overflow with forgiveness. The overflow was the pure fruit of the Spirit as the Amish visited the killer's family to comfort them on the day of the shootings. And at Charles Roberts's funeral, Amish mourners outnumbered the non-Amish.[3]

I share both of these true stories to make a crucial point. Forgiveness is possible even in the midst of the most traumatic and horrifying experiences. These examples should give us the courage to think in radical terms about our need to forgive the things we have suffered around the issue of race. The ability to forgive is made possible by the power of the Holy Spirit who indwells the heart of every believer. But that does not mean that it is easy.

> *We talk glibly about forgiving when we have never been injured; when we are injured, we know that it is not possible, apart from God's grace, for one human being to forgive another.* **—OSWALD CHAMBERS**

The father of one of the Amish children said this concerning forgiveness: "But you see," he said, "it's a journey. I still made that immediate choice in principle. But it took me a few years until I could feel that I really meant it inside me, to forgive Charlie."[4]

At the point when he did find the compassion, he said, "I felt a great weight falling off me. I felt lighter."[5]

I like that. And I believe that. Forgiveness makes you feel lighter. It warms the soul. It just feels right. It's a part of our Christian DNA to forgive. Scripture overflows with commandments about forgiveness:

- Bearing with one another, and forgiving each other, whoever has a complaint against anyone; just as the Lord forgave you, so also should you. (Col. 3:13)

- "Be on your guard! If your brother sins, rebuke him; and if he repents, forgive him. And if he sins against you seven times a day, and returns to you seven times, saying, 'I repent,' forgive him." (Luke 17:3–4)

- Let all bitterness and wrath and anger and clamor and slander be put away from you, along with all malice. Be kind to one another, tender-hearted, forgiving each other, just as God in Christ also has forgiven you. (Eph. 4:31–32)

- "And forgive us our debts, as we also have forgiven our debtors." (Matt. 6:12)

To forgive is to make a decision to cancel a debt that you are owed and not to hold it against your offender. There is no forgiveness without a debt. And when we realize the enormity of our own debt it makes forgiveness possible. So in this sense forgiveness is closely connected to gratitude. If our hearts overflow with gratitude for all that the Lord has done for us, all that He did to secure our salvation, all that He continues to do to keep us—then forgiveness will be easier. The person who doesn't have anything to be grateful for is an angry, vengeful person.

Jesus told the parable in Matthew 18 of a king who decided to collect the debts owed to him by his servants. One of these servants owed "ten thousand talents. . . . But since he did not have the means to repay, his lord commanded him to be sold along with his wife and children and all that he had, and repayment to be made. So the slave fell to the ground and prostrated himself before him, saying, 'Have patience with me and I will repay you everything.' And the lord of that slave felt compassion and released him and forgave him the debt" (vv. 24–27).

But later the same servant found another servant who owed him "a hundred denarii" and had him thrown into prison because he could not pay. When the king heard about what happened he became very angry. "You wicked slave. . . . Should you not also have had mercy . . . in the same way I had mercy on you?" (vv. 28, 32–33). The first servant was then thrown into prison because he refused to forgive.

The Lord's message is clear. We owe an enormous debt to God for our own sin—and He has already canceled our debt. We have a divine mandate to forgive everyone who offends us. To understand this puts us in the frame of mind to always be ready to offer forgiveness. Life is overflowing with opportunities for hurt and offense. To err is human . . . to forgive is divine.

BEYOND REVENGE: WHAT MANDELA DID

Many struggle to forgive because there's the notion that to forgive is to suggest that the wrong was not committed. But forgiveness requires an offense to have been committed. Someone was hurt. An evil deed was done. We saw how important this aspect of forgiveness is when watching South Africa come out of the evil system of apartheid.

The world watched with expectation when Nelson Mandela was inaugurated as the first democratically elected president of South Africa on May 10, 1994. His election marked the end of apartheid, a brutal system of oppression that separated whites and nonwhites by law and penalty of death. How would these "freed" blacks treat those who had oppressed them for years? Would there be a bloodbath? A civil war?

Nelson Mandela has been rightly celebrated. After being imprisoned for twenty-seven years many expected him to emerge consumed with a lust for revenge. But instead of spewing calls for revenge, he urged his people to work for reconciliation. He invited his former jailer to attend his presidential inauguration as a VIP guest. And instead of a bloodbath, the world saw the formation of the Truth and Reconciliation Commission (TRC). People who had committed the most heinous crimes were given amnesty in exchange for a full disclosure of the facts of the offense. Instead of revenge and retribution, this new nation chose to tread the difficult path of confession, forgiveness, and reconciliation.

The TRC allowed for the victims to share their stories and listen to the confessions of those who had victimized them. One of the speakers was the daughter of an African National Congress activist whom the police had ambushed and killed by mutilating his body before burning his car. When she came to the Truth and Reconciliation Commission to share her story, she revealed that the police were still harassing her mother and her children even after their father had died. After she had finished speaking, she was asked whether she would ever be able to forgive those who had done this. All eyes were on her as she spoke, "We would like to forgive. We just want to know whom to forgive."

And then there was Mrs. Savage, who was hurt by a hand

grenade in an attack that left her dependent on her children for bathing, clothing, and feeding. So much shrapnel remained in her body after surgery that she was unable to go through an airport security checkpoint. She was white; the perpetrator was black. But she told the Truth and Reconciliation Commission that she'd like to meet her attacker—in the spirit of forgiveness. She wanted to forgive him . . . and then, extraordinarily, she added, "And I hope he forgives me."[6]

There are many lessons about forgiveness that we can take from the events in South Africa. When a wrong has been done, the pain is real. It cannot be wished away or ignored. The costly act of forgiveness was essential for the victims as well as the perpetrators. Until forgiveness is given, the victim is literally tethered to their abusers.

A DECISION, NOT A FEELING

We've talked a lot about lamenting for our broken past and confessing our own part in the mess around race and religion. There's a lot of hurt and baggage around race for many of us. Maybe others were made to feel unwelcome in a church because they were the other. Maybe some were victimized by others because they are black or because they are white.

Whether we need to give forgiveness to the persons who have offended us, or whether we are in need of receiving forgiveness, God commands us to move from these places where we've been stuck. Whether we've been stuck for a short time or for generations, His command is that we move. That we don't wait until it feels right. We simply obey. Forgiveness is a decision of the will. It is not a feeling.

Corrie ten Boom's story of forgiveness demonstrates this so well. She and her sister, Betsie, had been prisoners in a Nazi camp during World War II. They were subjected to unspeakable treatment while there; her sister finally died due to her abuse. But Corrie survived and after the war devoted her life to helping to heal the hearts and lives of prisoners who had survived the Holocaust. She tells the story of what happened when she spoke at a church about the love of God and the power of forgiveness. As she looked out into the audience she saw the prison guard who had tortured her in prison. She hoped that he would leave as soon as the service was over, but he did not leave. Instead he waited for her, commending her on the message. And then he extended his hand to her and asked the question, "Would you forgive me?"

This is how Corrie describes what happened next:

> "'Jesus, help me!' I prayed silently. 'I can lift my hand. I can do that much. You supply the feeling.'"

> And so woodenly, mechanically, I thrust my hand into the one stretched out to me. And as I did, an incredible thing took place. The current started in my shoulder, raced down my arm, sprang into our joined hands. And then this healing warmth seemed to flood my whole being, bringing tears to my eyes.

> "I forgive you, brother!" I cried. "With all my heart!"

> For a long moment we grasped each other's hands, the former guard and the former prisoner. I had never known God's love so intensely as I did then."[7]

Surely the angels in heaven were rejoicing when Corrie chose to forgive. And I believe that they rejoice when believers choose to cancel the debt and embrace those who have wounded us.

The opposite response damages our very soul.

To choose forgiveness requires that we fight back our human desire for revenge. Revenge is dangerous because it's never really satisfied with an eye for an eye. Instead it rushes quickly into "punitive excess" taking much more from the offender than is due.[8]

When the apostle Paul wrote to the church in Rome he instructed them, "Never take your own revenge, beloved" (Rom. 12:19). Instead of seeking vengeance against those who persecuted them he urged them to "bless those who persecute you" (v. 14a). And then Paul explained exactly how they were to bless their enemies: "if your enemy is hungry, feed him, and if he is thirsty, give him a drink . . . " (v. 20).

As Nancy DeMoss Wolgemuth states, "When we fail to deal with hurts God's way, when we harbor resentment in our hearts, that bitterness—like an infection—will fester and work its way into our system, until ultimately we start viewing everything through the eyes of hurt—everything others do, everything that happens to us."[9] We begin to see every other black person or every other white person through the pain inflicted by someone else who was black or white.

Corrie ten Boom shared this concerning her work with those who were victims of the Holocaust: "Those who were able to forgive their former enemies were able also to return to the outside world and rebuild their lives, no matter what the physical scars. Those who nursed their bitterness re-mained invalids. It was as simple and as horrible as that."[10]

To forgive is divine. It makes us look like our heavenly Father. And we accomplish forgiveness through His Spirit living within us. There is no other way. But it is a choice that we must make individually to yield our right to strike back or to get even, and to instead offer forgiveness. To pardon our offender. It is a gift that we give to our offender and also to ourselves. There is no freedom like the freedom of forgiveness. It releases us from the ties that bind us to our offender and it puts us in a position to freely receive God's forgiveness and fellowship. It's beautiful.

FORGIVING MISSISSIPPI

When I moved to California I met whites who were very different from those in the South. The boss I worked for was white and he was kind to me. He appreciated my good work ethic and soon hired other people to work for me. These persons were also white. I became their boss, and we worked well together. They treated me with respect and I found myself beginning to shed the wall of unforgiveness and distrust that held my heart captive. I learned that I could love these people. But I continued to harbor unforgiveness in my heart for whites in Mississippi.

This selective forgiveness was challenged years later when I returned to Mississippi. After the events that transpired in Brandon, I had to make a choice. Would I allow my settled unforgiveness toward Mississippi whites to burn deeper into my soul or would I surrender to God's call to forgive? I was hurt and I was angry. I was caught in the struggle between the old man and the new man. When people spit in your face, it's nothing but the grace of God that keeps you from striking back. Revenge seemed fair and right . . . but love was the only way pleasing to God. I'm grateful to God because He kept me from making foolish decisions that would have most likely meant my life, and possibly the life of my family. Instead He pointed me in another direction toward forgiveness and love and I still marvel at the course my life has taken. I owe a debt of gratitude to God for overwhelming my fleshly desire for revenge and hate and giving me His supernatural grace of forgiveness.

I've always taken comfort from the Old Testament story of Joseph. We can learn much from Joseph's story of forgiveness. He had suffered repeatedly at the hands of his own brothers. Their bitterness and jealousy toward him had led them first

------

When people spit in your face, it's nothing but the grace of God that keeps you from striking back.

------

to throw him into a pit to die and later to sell him into slavery. He spent years exiled from his family and being at the mercy of a pharaoh. Yet when his brothers came to Egypt years later, bowing at his feet and begging for food to survive through the drought, Joseph had opportunity to finally exact justice. He could finally take revenge on them for how he had been mistreated. And if ever there was someone who could play the victim card, Joseph could have easily done that.

But instead he responds, "As for you, you meant evil against me, but God meant it for good, in order to bring about this present result, to preserve many people alive" (Gen. 50:20). These words have echoed throughout history as tribute to God's sovereignty. And they teach us that while we have no control over what others have done to us, we have complete control and responsibility for how we respond. God does much more than just give us the command to forgive. He gives us the enablement through the person of

109

the Holy Spirit. Each believer has within himself the same power "which He brought about in Christ, when He raised Him from the dead and seated Him at His right hand in the heavenly places" (Eph. 1:20). That is resurrection power. That is the power that is at work to conform us to His image. It empowers us to choose to forgive. Once again, forgiveness is a choice, not an emotion. It's a decision of the will.

Who would have imagined that apartheid in South Africa, the Holocaust, the shooting at Emanuel AME Church, and the shootings at the Amish school would be examples of anything but the most hideous wickedness? But God has chosen these unlikely circumstances as a model for how His people deal with the Enemy's sharpest arrows. God uses these dark, despairing events to show His awesome power. Against the stark contrast of the historical divide in the Church I'm praying for the glorious light of forgiveness to shine forth.

Oh, if the Church in America could be the next stage to platform His amazing grace! Oh, that we could be that place where the bridge is restored between black and white. Oh, if He could point to us as His victorious church, ushering in a new wave of believers who will storm the gates of hell, claiming those whose stubborn will has been broken by our witness. If we could truly forgive one another and begin to produce the works of repentance, He would be glorified. In the next chapter, we will see what that repentance might look like.

PRAYER · Oh Lord, our God. This thing about forgiveness is hard for us. Because of that, many of us have chosen to neglect it. We have allowed bitterness to well up in our hearts and it has choked out Your power in our lives. Help us to make the decision of the will to forgive. And then, Lord, would You step in with Your overwhelming power to activate our hearts? Help us to forgive others just as You have forgiven us, Father. Help us to heal from our hurts so that we can be the church that points the world to You.

TEAR DOWN THIS WALL!

"Therefore bear fruit in keeping with repentance." —MATTHEW 3:8

The movie *Woodlawn* is a beautiful story of how the gospel sparked a spiritual awakening that tore down walls of hate and prejudice in Birmingham, Alabama, in 1973. Violence in the city was so rampant because of integration and busing that the FBI considered closing Woodlawn High School. But there was a chaplain who shared the gospel with the football team. Almost every player accepted Christ as Savior. After finding a "white power" sign behind the gym, the chaplain challenged them that "Jesus, and what's written on this paper cannot coexist."

What happened next is a true story of forgiveness, repentance, and transformation. The players decided to love one another. They linked arms, black and white players together— and God did the miraculous. Black and white players were seen fellowshipping together at home meetings through the Fellowship of Christian Athletes. The coach accepted Christ when he saw what was happening with his players. And the revival spread through the entire city of Birmingham.[1] Repentance is the most beautiful demonstration of the power of Christ in the life of the believer. I believe that repentance begins with a consciousness that something is wrong. I think the conscience gets louder if I ignore it. There's an awareness that my life is contradicting itself. I'm not living up to what I know is right. I've become a hypocrite. The apostle Paul said it like this: "Wretched man that I am! Who will set me free from the body of this death? Thanks be to God through Jesus Christ our Lord! So then, on the one hand I myself with my mind am serving the law of God, but on the other, with my flesh the law of sin" (Rom. 7:24–25).

Repentance is a commitment to turn from sin to works of obedience. In the New Testament the word for repent, *metanoia*, means "a change of mind" or "regret/remorse." In Matthew 3, John the Baptist rebukes the Pharisees and the Sadducees because they claim to have Abraham as their father but their behavior shows no sign that they know Abraham or the God of Abraham. If they knew Abraham they would have welcomed the message of John the Baptist and would have eagerly received the Messiah. He challenges them to repent of their evil ways and demonstrate their repentance with a change in their actions.

There's a beautiful demonstration of repentance in Luke 19 when Jesus encountered a very rich tax collector as he was passing through Jericho. After calling to Zaccheus to come down from a tree so that He could go home with him, Jesus reveals the truth of the gospel to this sinner. Zaccheus was so convicted by the message of salvation and so grateful to be a recipient that he eagerly proclaimed, "Behold, Lord, half of my possessions I will give to the poor, and if I have defrauded anyone of anything, I will give back four times as much" (v. 8). Zaccheus is a model for us of what it looks like to produce works that indicate repentance. We learn from his example that repentance should be evidenced by a change in behavior. We owe a debt to those we have harmed directly or indirectly by our actions or our silence on the issue of reconciliation.

If we have been silent and have chosen to ignore the mistreatment of others in the past, we should begin to speak up and challenge injustices. If we were racist and bigoted in our speech and actions, there should be a radical change that is observable. If we have been angry and spiteful toward the other, there should be a radical change that is observable. And, yes, if we have an abundance of wealth and we have the opportunity to use this blessing to encourage those we have previously been prejudiced against, we should open our hands in Christian love and brotherhood. We should tear down the walls that have separated us for so long.

When I think of tearing down walls I'm reminded of President Ronald Reagan's challenge to Mikhail Gorbachev to tear down the Berlin Wall. The wall had been built in 1961 to prevent Germans from escaping the Communist regime of East Germany to the freedom of West Germany. When President Reagan stood at the wall in 1987 he said, *"Es gibt nur ein Berlin."* *There is only one Berlin.* He then said the words that led to one of his most important accomplishments as president: "Mr. Gorbachev, tear down this wall!"[2]

Those words are appropriate for us today as we think about the church in America. *There is only one Church.* There is only one blood. And just as the Berlin Wall was torn down, brick by brick, we must all work together to tear down the walls of suspicion, racism, and hatred that have divided us. We have been intentional about building the walls that separate us as blacks and whites. We must be even more intentional about tearing them down.

ENGAGING THE "OTHER" IN EVERYDAY LIFE

But what does that look like in everyday life? On an individual level we can begin thinking about where and how we engage the other in the normal course of life. Is it at a grocery store, a doctor's office, at a school? In our busyness as a culture we have forgotten the social graces of smiling and speaking to one another. So here's a good place to start. Ask a new acquaintance their name and write it down so that the next time you see them you can refer to them by name. There's something about calling another person by name that shows honor and deference. Experts have suggested that to remember a person's name communicates respect and acceptance.

———

Tearing down the walls we've built also means that we speak differently of "them."

———

In his "Tearing Down Walls" sermon series, Dave Stone, senior pastor of Southeast Christian Church in Louisville, Kentucky, shared what happened when an African American family joined his friend's church in Louisville in the 1980s. Shortly after the family joined, the wife began attending some of the women's events. After one of the meetings, a member innocently said to her, "Margaret, it's so good to have you. I don't want to say the wrong thing, so tell me, do you prefer to be called African American, Black, or Negro?" Margaret looked at her and smiled. "I think I'd just like to be called Margaret."[3]

Whether it's the new family who just integrated your neighborhood or the couple who just visited your church for the first time, don't miss the opportunity to extend your hand in welcome and greeting. Express an interest in them by asking questions about what they like to do or about their family. Pray for opportunities to interact on a regular basis.

Repentance and tearing down the walls we've built also means that we speak differently of "them." "Bless those who curse you, pray for those who mistreat you" (Luke 6:28). To bless means to speak well of. This biblical command can radically change our interaction within our circle of friends. When the topic of the "other" comes up, we have the opportunity to change the discourse. Rather than the toxic communication that often arises when "those people" are discussed, we are challenged to speak well of those who are being demonized.

True repentance requires that we lovingly confront our brothers and sisters concerning racial sins and personal bigotry. And this is the perfect time to put this principle into practice: "In everything, therefore, treat people the same way you want them to treat you, for this is the Law and the Prophets" (Matt. 7:12).

We need to get beyond our ignorance of the other. We need to move beyond the thinking that white privilege means that all whites live a privileged life. This perspective ignores the reality of class in this country. The plight of poor whites was largely ignored until the last presidential election. According to the 2013 data from the US Department of Agriculture, 40.2 percent of food stamp recipients were white; 25.7 percent, black.[4]

What's Their Story?

We would do well to hear and learn from the stories of whites, especially those who share the common struggle of poverty and marginalization. In *Hillbilly Elegy*, J. D. Vance shares his story of growing up poor: "To these folks, poverty is the family tradition—their ancestors were day laborers in the Southern slave economy, sharecroppers after that, coal miners after that, and machinists and millworkers during more recent times. Americans call them hillbillies, rednecks, or white trash. I call them neighbors, friends, and family."[5] When we understand the details of the other's story we realize that we have much more in common than we ever imagined. Shared story is how we build friendship.

There is a touching scene in Kathryn Stockett's *The Help* that illustrates this point. Miss Celia refers to her maid, Minny Jackson, as her friend. Minny is troubled by Miss Celia's lack of understanding about how things are supposed to be between blacks and whites in the South. But Miss Celia is persistent in breaking down the walls. She shows great respect for Minny by paying her well and asking for lessons in home-making. She even has lunch with Minny in the kitchen rather than at the big table and asks her how she's doing. Minny is finally persuaded that Celia's friendship is real when she arrives at the house for work and finds that Celia has cooked a complete meal for her. She takes a seat at the table, and Celia serves her. This role reversal stemmed from Celia's memory of her upbringing. She had come from the poor side of the tracks, so she knew how it felt to be ignored and treated as if she were invisible or, worse yet, unworthy. This experiential knowledge of what it meant to be poor served as a bridge over the dividing wall between black and white.[6]

If all we know of ourselves is what we learned in history books, what we observe on the nightly news or read in the newspaper, we are missing out on key information. American textbooks were written with a specific bias that reinforces the systemic evil of racism. For that reason, important contributions from blacks leading to advances in science, technology, and other areas of American life were omitted. A prominent textbook publisher was challenged for suggesting that "African slaves came to the US as economic migrants."[7] And the media has done its job of portraying the black man in particular as dangerous, violent, and deserving of incarceration. These portrayals reinforce stereotypes in our minds that fuel self-hatred and anger. We must become advocates for telling our stories to our children, so that they understand the wealth of our history in this country. We must reclaim the oral tradition of our ancestors. We must instill pride in our children and faith that our God can make much of their lives just as He did for many of our forebears. And we must help quell the anger that overflows in many of our ethnic communities. We must help them reach across the divide and love others regardless of color.

Because American history for the most part omits the contributions of African Americans, it is important for white Christians to be intentional about learning the history and the experience of blacks in this country. There are many ways to arrive at this experience. We need to be sensitive to the Holy Spirit's leading as He may direct us in unexpected ways into the path of the other. Visiting a black church, volunteering at an inner-city school, or helping out at a senior citizens' home are just a few possibilities. These experiences provide opportunities for us to get to know the other's story. Getting to know the stories behind the statistics can go a long way in helping remove the barriers and pull down stereotypes and prejudices. As Soong-Chan Rah wrote, "The best stories will inspire change in the listener. Stories tell us about the story-teller. They invite us into another world and challenge us to envision a world beyond our own."[8]

The Evangelical Covenant Church denomination offers several immersion experiences that are excellent opportunities to learn. One of them is the Sankofa Journey: "an intentional, cross-racial prayer journey that seeks to assist disciples of Christ on their move toward a righteous response to the social ills related to racism. This interactive experience explores historic sites of importance in the Civil Rights

---

"Discussions about power are usually avoided by those who have it."

SOONG-CHAN RAH

---

movement, and sites of oppression and inequality for people of color, while seeking to move participants toward healing the wounds and racial divide caused by hundreds of years of racial injustice in the United States."[9] *Sankofa* is an African word from the Akan tribe of Ghana that is translated as, "it is not taboo to fetch what is at risk of being left behind."[10] It embraces the idea of looking back in order to move forward.

I highly recommend a visit to the Smithsonian National Museum of African American History and Culture in Washington, D.C. The museum tells the American story through the African American lens. Established by an act of Congress in 2003, it is the only national museum devoted exclusively to the documentation of African American life, history, and culture. Early childhood programs at the institution are built around the statement by Frederick Douglass: "It's easier to build strong children than to repair broken men."

Privilege and Power

As part of the repentance journey, we will need to talk about the issues of privilege and power. I agree with Soong-Chan Rah: "For many American evangelicals, discussions about power seem sordid or out of place in a Christian context. However, discussions about power are usually avoided by those who have it—they don't want to discuss the dynamic lest doing so leads to a power shift. But we need to talk about these realities."[11]

In *The Nature of Prejudice*, famed sociologist Gordon Allport offered a social science theory that was foundational in the thinking of Martin Luther King Jr. and the *Brown v. Board of Education* decision. A key point in his argument was that "prejudice (unless deeply rooted in the character structure of the individual) may be reduced by equal status contact between majority and minority groups in the pursuit of common goals."[12] The truth according to Scripture is that the blood of Jesus Christ places us all on equal status. At the foot of the cross where He shed His precious blood there is no rich, no poor, no Jew or Gentile, no male or female—no black and no white. Power dynamics are out of place in the church. We must live according to these biblical truths.

A wonderful way to engage this part of the journey may be by attending an ethnic church or social club for a significant period of time and becoming a learner. If your city has a branch of the NAACP or the National Urban League, make it a point to attend meetings. Become a part of that community. Learn by observing and listening. In a perfect world, we could just get into each other's skin and experience what life is like on the other side. We can't do that, but we can ask questions that indicate an interest in learning more rather than challenging leadership. Learn by experiencing what it feels like to be a minority.

Something wonderful happened in early 2017 after the killing of Alton Sterling by a white man, the killing of Philando Castile by a Latino, and the killing of five police officers in Dallas by a black man. Rev. Lee Jenkins, the black pastor of Eagles Nest Church in Roswell, Georgia, reached across the divide to Matt Miller, the white pastor of Roswell Community Church, and asked to meet together to talk about race. Within seven months the two had become two hundred. They began by viewing the movie *Selma* and met in small groups reflecting on the movie and discussing the things we assume about the other race. The small groups met in individual homes, and for many of the whites it was the first time they had ever been in a black home. The discussion was raw, from the talk of having grown up in the South where "The n-word was used not as an insult, but as an adjective;" and the perception that whites think they're better than everybody else. After meeting in one another's homes for seven months and spending time together, real relationships have been forged. The two churches continue to have "Conversations" about grace and race once a month.[13]

When a Neighborhood "Changes"

Much has been said about gentrification, which takes place when middle-class or affluent people restore and upgrade urban communities and move in. For some time this movement has been seen as a key step in accomplishing reconciliation. However, local residents usually see gentrification quite differently. The *Urban Dictionary* defines gentrification in this way: "When 'urban renewal' of lower class neighbourhoods with condos attracts yuppie tenants, driving up rents and driving out long time, lower income residents. It often begins with influxes of local artists looking for a cheap place to live, giving the neighbourhood a bohemian flair. This hip reputation attracts yuppies who want to live in such an atmosphere, driving out the lower income artists and lower income residents, often ethnic/racial minorities, changing the social character of the neighbourhood."[14]

If your church is considering moving out of the neighborhood to escape those who don't look like you, this is an opportunity for you to speak truth to power.

In a recent post, "More on Leaving White Evangelicalism: A Response from Bryan Loritts,"[15] Pastor Bryan Loritts argues that church planters who start churches in gentrifying neighborhoods should consider learning from and partnering with existing minority churches. There's a lot of cultural capital and experience that they can benefit from. Unless gentrification has a clear, intentional goal of living among those native to the urban environment and forging meaningful relationships, it falls short of what is essential to accomplish reconciliation.

And finally, repentance may mean rethinking a decision, as an individual or as a local church, to relocate because the neighborhood is "changing." Perhaps the changes in the neighborhood are God's way of bringing the harvest of souls within reach of your church, providing an evangelistic opportunity and helping the local church look more like the church was intended to look. When Jesus said that the harvest is ripe but the laborers are few, He was lamenting the fact that believers are not eager to share their faith and take His message to the lost. If your church is considering moving out of the neighborhood to escape those who don't look like you, this is an opportunity for you to speak truth to power. There are countless examples in Scripture of those who were bold enough to speak the truth to those in power. Nathan was bold in confronting King David about his wrongdoing. God used him to bring David to a place of brokenness and obedience. Who knows but that you are strategically placed where you are for God to use you to turn hearts toward His purposes.

Brian Clark, the pastor of Riverside Presbyterian Church in Sterling, Virginia, shares how his church handled a similar opportunity:

> Church members became aware that the demographics of neighborhoods near the church were changing. Most notably, about 14 percent of the population was Hispanic.
> "That's a significant part of the community," he [Clark] said. In discerning how to better serve that population, Riverside eventually decided to add a co-pastor, the Rev. Edwin Andrade, who leads worship services in Spanish. Clark conducts services in English.[16]

The church also provides meeting space for Boy Scouts, Girl Scouts, and for twelve-step organizations to meet. They have partnered with a local school to help students from low-income families and are working with a sister church to minister to immigrant day laborers.[17]

What happened at Riverside is one of the most organic ways for the church to become a multicultural church. By simply accommodating and welcoming the changing demographics of the neighborhood they are modeling biblical reconciliation. More than anything else I believe that this is what God is looking for in the Church today to turn the hearts of unbelievers to Himself. I get excited when I think about a new wave of churches that buck the historic trend of moving farther and farther out into suburbia to escape the changing realities of their community. As more and more churches make this radical decision to stay and trust God to show them how to meet the need and have the right heart to love their neighbor we will see the fulfillment of His grand vision on earth.

Ed Gilbreath's insightful interview with senior pastor Peter Ahn (KA) of Metro CC in Englewood, New Jersey, and senior pastor Alex Gee (AA) of Fountain of Life CC in Madison, Wisconsin, offers recommendations of how to move forward in the church on the issue of reconciliation. 1) Pastors must preach against racism in spite of the risk of losing their popularity; and 2) Denominations and churches must choose leaders "who have experience in multiethnic ministry and dialogue."[18]

Repentance is about change. It's evidenced by a change in relationship from enemy to friend. And most importantly, this effort is empowered and energized by the person of the Holy Spirit. He is actively engaged because this pleases the heart of the Father. I pray that we all find ourselves moving along the journey from enemies to friends and true brothers and sisters in Christ.

PRAYER · Lord, when we think of change
it can be unsettling. We often choose
to remain unchanged because we are
comfortable with what we have been doing.
Change takes us into the unknown. Help
us to trust You to guide us to repentance.

Make us uncomfortable with superficial relationships. Give us boldness to speak to our friends as they voice racist statements. Give us courage to reach out to those who we have never befriended before. Show us, Lord, how to be friends with our brothers and sisters. Show us how to be one, Lord. For Your glory.

LIVING IT OUT

Water of Life
Community Church
LEAD PASTOR: Dan Carroll

FONTANA, CALIFORNIA

We are located in Fontana, California. We are a nondenominational Christian church that began in my home as a Bible study in 1990. We started with twenty-seven adults and fifteen kids, and at this point we have 7,500 people per weekend. The decision to become multicultural was really made in my heart when we first began. There were a number of factors that drew me in that direction. I grew up in an African American community and played basketball for an African American coach in college. I've been on the Fontana Police Department's Minority Hiring Commission and also taught at a black high school at one point in time. My desire to connect with and better understand my students led me to study black history. All of these things heightened my awareness of the beauty of the history and culture of African Americans.

I also went on the mission field with Youth with a Mission. I lived in Malaysia and God gave me a heart for nations and different people groups. So when I came home to the US and planted Water of Life, it was always in my heart that we would and should be multicultural. But it didn't start out like that. When our church first started we were a very, very white church. In my heart I grieved about this because I knew this did not agree with God's desire for his church. I went before the Lord and just cried out to Him and said, "Lord, help us. I love other nationalities, tongues, and tribes, and nations. Please give us other people."

I think that a multicultural church is a biblical church. At Water of Life we talk about loving every tongue, and tribe, and nation, and every culture, and honoring what God has put in cultures and different people groups. We believe that God's image can be found in every people group and that we need to look for places to honor His presence in culture and in people. The word *ekteno* used in 1 Peter 4:8 means to "fervently love one another"—is a very important word. It means to stretch out in our love for other people. I speak to my staff about it often and how important it is to love people—and love other people outside your comfort zone. We do that with African Americans. We do that with Latinos. We do that with Asians.

So we have been very intentional about making Water of Life feel like 'home' to different people. Even going so far as telling our hospitality people that if there was an African American walking next to a white person, reach around the white person and greet the African American first. I did that just to try to honor people. To try to make a statement. I was always very conscious of who was on our stage. And how they were presented. So that minorities would feel like they had a place in our church.

Throughout the years when we've had African Americans leading worship or on our staff—we have many, many African Americans on our staff as pastors or leaders—we made sure that people understood that there is no ceiling. So qualified people can gravitate to the top. We have several African American, Latino, and Asian elders. We made sure that we had pastors who represented other ethnicities. The communication is very clear to our church that this is a high priority and that we are a mixed culture.

The process we used to become multicultural really was a hit-and-miss kind of a deal. I have spoken openly about racism and minority issues for the last twenty-eight years. We began by openly talking about race in our classes and in the places where we have different gatherings. We made that a point. We talked about what it's like to be African American, what it's like to be Latino, what it's like to be a minority. We speak openly about those things in our messages and in our classes because we want people to feel safe. We want them to know that we care about them and we are not embarrassed at any level to have other people.

It took a while to convince people that this was really our heart. But after staying in, and staying in, and staying in, we won people over and they began to trust us. We cried out to God many years ago and asked Him to send us people—and He did. I guess that our church is today about 40 percent Latino, and probably 25 percent white, probably 28–30 percent African American, and 5 percent Asian. We have a lot of Filipinos, a lot of Asians from Southeast Asia, a lot of Chinese, and we are a really blessed people. So we are grateful that we reflect the kingdom of God and we reflect the heart of the Father.

GOD DON'T WANT NO COWARD SOLDIERS

Therefore, since we have so great a cloud of witnesses surrounding us, let us also lay aside every encumbrance and the sin which so easily entangles us, and let us run with endurance the race that is set before us, fixing our eyes on Jesus, the author and perfecter of faith, who for the joy set before Him endured the cross, despising the shame, and has sat down at the right hand of the throne of God. For consider Him who has endured such hostility by sinners against Himself, so that you will not grow weary and lose heart. —HEBREWS 12:1-3

I'm often asked this question: "John Perkins, why did you stay in the fight for social justice? Why didn't you give up?" Most people would say I was committed to justice, probably because my first book was *Let Justice Roll Down*. But as I have grown in my faith it's been more than that. I wanted to keep it within the gospel, trying to fill those holes up that we pulled out. We're asking questions now that should never be asked: "Does life matter?" What are you talking about? All life matters!

My father's life mattered, even though he didn't know

how to read or write and had to put an X on the grocery bill. My brother's life mattered, even though he was killed. And my mother's life mattered, even though she died of pellagra. When I wanted to quit, my memories of them wouldn't let me. Their memories stay with me and drive me to work for a holistic gospel.

And I think that when the Lord puts fire in your belly and a call on your life, quitting isn't an option. But if we're able to stand and to remain committed, it's because of His grace. We can't claim credit for it. He does it in us and through us by the power of the Holy Spirit. Our part is to just do what He tells us to do.

I love the book of Hebrews. It's full of encouragement. The writer calls the roll of believers who God used to accomplish His purposes. They were the vessels who moved the story of Scripture along: Abel, Enoch, Noah, Abraham, Sarah, Isaac, Jacob, Joseph, Moses, Rahab, Gideon, Barak, Samson, Jephthah, David, Samuel, and the prophets. The common ingredient for each of them was faith. They were bold enough to take God at His Word and to trust Him to fulfill it. They give meaning to James's argument that "faith without works is dead." And they challenge those who think that faith is something that you hold in your head without acting on it.

We all need to take God at His Word and believe that He is engaged in the effort to bring His Church together as one. The persons in the Hall of Faith in Hebrews were set apart from everyone else because they chose to trust in God. For many of them, their faith put their lives at risk. For others, like Noah, their trust in God saved their own life and the lives of many others.

"MY MIND WAS COMPLETELY MADE UP FOR ABOLITION"

Over the course of history there have been a lot of folks God used to move the issue of reconciliation forward. Their stories of great faith are an encouragement to keep fighting and never give up. One of those individuals was William Wilberforce. When we saw the movie *Amazing Grace* we were thrilled by his life. Now that was a picture of commitment!

John Wesley wrote a letter to Wilberforce on February 24, 1791 just six days before Wesley passed away. In that letter he said, "Unless God has raised you up for this very thing, you will be worn out by the opposition of men and devils. But if God be for you, who can be against you? Are all of them stronger than God? O be not weary of well-doing! Go on, in the name of God and in the power of His might, till even American slavery (the vilest that ever saw the sun) shall vanish away before it."[1]

Wilberforce was elected to Parliament in 1780, but he sensed God calling him to fight against slavery on Easter of 1786. This is what he said about that call: "So enormous, so dreadful, so irremediable did the trade's wickedness appear that my own mind was completely made up for abolition. Let the consequences be what they would: I from this time determined that I would never rest until I had effected its abolition."[2] I like that! This is God's amazing power at work in the lives of people who will answer the call.

By 1805 Wilberforce and Thomas Clarkson had introduced twenty resolutions to end slavery. Each one was defeated. Wilberforce came under attack again and again, but his efforts finally paid off in 1807. Parliament finally abolished the slave trade in the British Empire. Wilberforce continued working to make sure the slave trade laws were enforced and the trade was finally abolished. He became a prominent member of the Clapham Sect, a group of devout Christians of influence in government and business. I think about what it must have taken for him to keep on keeping on, year after year, defeat after defeat. I don't think it was anything but faith in God and believing that He could do the impossible.

A MARTYR IN FREEDOM'S CAUSE

As the message of freedom made its way to the shores of America it captured the heart of Elijah Parish Lovejoy. His martyrdom was one of the key events that led to the Civil War. He was born in Albion, Maine, in 1802. After graduating from Waterville College in 1826 he went to teach school in St. Louis. He joined the First Presbyterian Church. After experiencing a call to the ministry, he studied at Princeton Theological Seminary and later served as pastor of a church in St. Louis. He used his religious newspaper, the *St. Louis Observer*, to protest against slavery. His argument became stronger after he witnessed a slave, Francis J. McIntosh, being burned at the stake. Soon his publication drew the anger and rage of Southern slaveholders. He was forced to escape to the free state of Illinois after his printing press was destroyed by a mob in July 1836.[3]

In Alton he became pastor of the College Avenue Presbyterian Church and engaged in the antislavery cause. Though he was in a free state, his new publication, the *Alton Observer* was soon under attack. He would suffer the loss of three more printing presses before the fateful night of November 7, 1837. On that night, twenty of his supporters joined him to make sure his new press would be kept safe until it could be installed at the *Observer*. A large crowd began to gather outside, and soon things became violent. As Lovejoy went to try to put out a fire that had been set on the roof of the building, he was shot five times and killed. The mob then rushed the building, found the press, and threw it out a window to the riverbank. In his biography of Lovejoy, former US Senator from Illinois Paul Simon wrote that Lovejoy was a man "whose death would electrify the nation."[4]

"I SEE FREEDOM IN THE AIR"

We have been blessed by God to have had in our own time men and women who have this same spirit of commitment and sacrifice to stay the course in spite of discouragement and opposition. None of them were perfect, yet God was able to use each of them for His purposes in glorious ways. Any Hall of Faith for reconciliation has to include Dr. Martin Luther King Jr. His life inspired countless men and women to work fearlessly to bring blacks and whites together and to break down the barriers that separated us. It's hard to say what his most valuable contribution to the cause was. It may have been his willingness to be jailed and abused for the cause. He demonstrated with his life that this work was worthy of great personal sacrifice.

His work for the poor and efforts to end bus segregation and secure voting rights showed the world that the gospel requires us to serve the needs of the least of us. His principles of nonviolent resistance taught generations of people that Christ's way of turning the other cheek is powerful. It allows God to move on our behalf. And his letter from a Birmingham jail to the white pastors showed his willingness to reach across the divide and have meaningful conversation: "The purpose of our direct-action program is to create a situation so crisis-packed that it will inevitably open the door to nego-tiation. I therefore concur with you in your call for negotia-tion. Too long has our beloved Southland been bogged down in a tragic effort to live in monologue rather than dialogue."[5] His speech from the March on Washington let us all get a glimpse of what could be.

When he preached to garbage workers in Memphis the night before he was killed, he spoke of the commitment that had held the struggle together. When Bull Connor set the dogs on the marchers they would sing, "Ain't gonna let no-body turn me around." When he turned the fire hoses on pro-testers, they would sing "Over my head I see freedom in the air." And when those demonstrating peacefully were thrown into paddy wagons they would sing, "We Shall Overcome." He said, ". . . when people get caught up with that which is right and they are willing to sacrifice for it, there is no stop-ping point short of victory."[6]

Dr. King made the ultimate sacrifice when his life was snuffed out by a bullet on April 4, 1968. His life was that seed that is planted and brings forth much fruit—multiply-ing fruit. "Truly, truly, I say to you, unless a grain of wheat falls into the earth and dies, it remains alone; but if it dies, it bears much fruit" (John 12:24). So many of us were inspired by his life and by his death to believe that this work is worth sacrificing for.

MORE HEROES IN THE TRENCHES

My friend Bill Pannell is another one of those heroes. In 1968 he wrote *My Friend, the Enemy*. It shook the evangelical world. Many of his white friends who read the book did not believe that he wrote it, because the life that he wrote about was foreign to them. What it revealed was that "it was possible for a white person to call Bill a close friend and still know little of a black man's life in a white world."[7] A few years later in 1971, Bill became Fuller Theological Seminary's first African American trustee.

When asked what has sustained him over these many years in the struggle for reconciliation he says that it is "the realization that God chose me."[8] That realization has kept Bill in the trenches for now more than sixty-eight years, fighting for reconciliation in spite of very little change. In 2014, after nearly fifty years of engagement at Fuller, the African American Studies department was named after him: the William E. Pannell Center for African American Studies. As professor emeritus of preaching at Fuller he continues to this day to be a bridge.

Tom Skinner spoke to us about reading the Bible and discovering that there are more than three thousand verses that speak of the poor.

Another one of those heroes was Tom Skinner. He was raised in Harlem and in his early life was a gang leader. After becoming a believer, he left the gangs and by the providence of God was able to leave without severe consequences. God's call on his life was evident as his evangelistic ministry spread across the United States and the Caribbean. He wrote *How Black Is the Gospel?* to call all Christians—blacks, whites, conservatives, and liberals—together to do the work of the Church. He worked alongside William Pannell and often worked with Billy Graham.

Tom was a hard-hitting critic of racism in American culture. He exercised great influence on young black Christian leaders. He was a bridge between the black and white evangelical communities. When it became clear that the National Association of Evangelicals did not intend to address social concerns, Tom worked with others to organize the National Black Evangelical Association. While some black evangelicals insisted that disengagement was the right thing to do, Tom insisted that it was important to work from within, as fellow believers.[9]

He worked with James Earl Massey, and many others who were all influenced by Martin Luther King Jr. and were convinced that reconciliation was "God's one-item agenda"[10] for the Church. When he spoke to the Christian Community Development Association (CCDA) in 1990, he spoke to us about reading the Bible and discovering that there are more than three thousand verses that speak of the poor. He was motivated by God's heart for the poor to preach the truth to power whether people wanted to hear it or not. He argued that God intended for the tithe to be used to feed and serve the poor, but instead we give the tithe back to ourselves and use it to build new buildings and serve ourselves.[11]

Bishop George D. McKinney, founder of the St. Stephens Church of God in Christ in San Diego, California, was another one who worked hard in the early years for the cause of reconciliation and justice. He was a friend of Billy Graham and helped to desegregate the Graham revivals in the 1950s and 1960s. He speaks about how hard it was in the early years to get black pastors to believe that Graham was trustworthy. Only a few would attend meetings at St. Stephens in the early years. But in 2003 when the Graham Crusade returned to San Diego, St. Stephens was overflowing with congregants eager

to hear the Word. God had used His servant McKinney to
make great progress with reconciliation. On March 7, 2001,
the National Association of Evangelicals (NAE), presented
Bishop McKinney with a Racial Reconciliation Man of the
Year Award. At the age of eighty-seven he continues to pastor
the St. Stephens Church and fight for reconciliation.[12]

The National Black Evangelical Association was committed in the early years to taking the evangelical message to the
black community and dealing with social problems. While
white evangelicals were debating whether Martin Luther King
Jr. was a Christian or not, those of us in the black community
were energized by his message and determined to make a
difference in our communities. Any roll call for reconciliation
must include the names of those early heroes: Rev. Aaron M.
Hamlin, Mother Dessie Webster, Rev. Marvin Prentis, Bishop
William C. Holman, Rev. Jeremiah Rowe, Rev. William H.
Bentley, Missionary Ruth Lewis Bentley, Rev. Howard Jones,
Rev. Charles Williams, Rev. Tom Skinner, and Dr. Tony
Evans. Most of these individuals were highly educated and
influential. That God would allow me to rub shoulders with
any of them is most humbling.

Rev. Marvin Levy Prentis was the first chairman of
the board and the first president of this association, the
NBEA. He worked side by side with William H. Bentley, a
Chicago-based minister-theologian (and Fuller Seminary
graduate) who provided steady and strategic leadership.
During Bentley's presidency he worked hard to explain Blackness as a gift from God that is worthy of respect and dignity.
The association revolved around two key themes, fellowship
and ministry. The organization became a place where black
evangelicals—many of whom were engaging in white evan-

gelical circles—could find a place of genuine fellowship and community. He wrote the chapter on "Black Believers in the Black Community" for the book *The Evangelicals*, which David F. Wells and John D. Woodbridge edited. That chapter explained that black evangelicalism was rooted in the theology of the Bible school movement, which had educated most of the more prominent African American evangelicals. The chapter also explained why blacks had been so quick to act in the social arena and how black evangelical pastors could bring change in white denominations.[13]

LINKING ARMS IN THE STRUGGLE

I want to lift up a number of white evangelicals that God allowed us to work more closely with in the early years. Dr. Vernon Grounds was the president of Denver Seminary for many years. He became a dear friend and one who willingly undergirded our work. When I came on campus he would call a meeting of two or three hundred seminary students for chapel. They supported me at a time when there was a need for a black voice. Dr. Grounds and I became good friends.

During the 1960s Grounds insisted that evangelicals combine social action with personal conversion. He wrote *Evangelicalism and Social Responsibility* in 1969 declaring that the Savior's love for humanity must compel believers to be involved in social justice. The Vernon Grounds Institute of Public Ethics at Denver Seminary was instituted to carry forward his commitment to social justice. It has been said that "without the contributions of Vernon Grounds to social justice and Christian counseling, evangelicalism as we know it would not exist."[14]

Another like-minded individual was Paul Jewitt of Fuller

Theological Seminary. He was a professor at Fuller, and he became a good friend and a partner in the struggle for reconciliation. He joined the movement, not as a leader, but as a supporter. He was strong in his belief that all people regardless of race or gender were equal and were created in the image of God—that God doesn't have any stepchildren. Paul used his influence at Fuller to teach the truth about prejudice in America and to help provide context for the racial strife of the '60s.

Rufus Jones, president of the Conservative Baptist Home Mission Society, also was active in pushing for reconciliation. He believed that the Christian faith had to include social justice. He rejected the feeling of some folks that social action was dirty work for devout believers. Rufus worked closely with Ron Sider, Paul Henry, Ron Potter, and others to call together about forty or so of us in Chicago in 1973. What came out of that meeting was the Chicago Declaration. The purpose was to call evangelicals to biblical social concern.

God expects us to stay on the wall and not quit until the battle is won.

A key part of that declaration included this statement: "We affirm that God abounds in mercy and that he forgives all who repent and turn from their sins. So we call our fellow evangelical Christians to demonstrate repentance in a Christian discipleship that confronts the social and political injustice of our nation."[15] (A full copy of the Chicago Declaration can be found online at: http://www.evangelicalsforsocialaction.org/

about-esa/history/chicago-declaration-of-evangelical-social-concern/).

There was a lot of pushback when this statement was released. Some even suggested that the signers of the declaration were socialists or communists. But I'm grateful for those who were bold enough to challenge where we were and to look forward to where God might take us together.

Each of these individuals did their part to move the vision of reconciliation forward. Without them the chain would be broken and progress, as slow as it has been, would have stopped. The same is true with you. You are a link in the chain of progress, and our children and their children are depending on each one of us to remain strong, to do our part until the work is finally done. And one day it will be done. Of that I am confident.

I love them for their personal sacrifice to push for justice for all. I believe the Lord calls each of us to do the same. To do our part, in our corner of the world, trusting Him to make the difference. I often think of this work that we're called to do as being soldiers in God's army. An old spiritual, "We Are Soldiers in the Army," proclaims, "We are soldiers in the army. We have to fight although we have to cry. We've got to hold up the bloodstained banner. We've got to hold it up until we die!"

I believe that's what God expects of us: to stay on the wall and not quit until the battle is won. It's hard to get people to sign on these days to that kind of commitment. Most people have retirement and ease on their minds and want nothing more than to be able to sit down and just enjoy life. I understand that. The urge to rest and enjoy life is a strong one. But the Lord talked about working while it is day because night comes when no man can work. Wilberforce, Lovejoy, King,

Skinner, Bentley, Grounds, Jewett—each one worked until the Lord called him home from labor to reward. I am convinced that this work of reconciliation is worth sacrificing all of life for.

What then shall we say about this Hall of Faith? Some mentioned were rich; some were poor—by birth or by choice. Some were black; some were white. Some were men; some were women. Some were educated; others could not read or write. Some were well known; others were easily overlooked. That God chose to use each of them is proof that He is no respecter of persons. Faith is the single human quality needed for God to do great things.

If we believe that God's vision for the church is one unified body, loving one another with the same love that Jesus and the Father shared, then we must acknowledge that the Enemy has been hard at work to destroy that vision. If we didn't know the end of the story this could be discouraging, depressing news. But we know that in the end God wins. His purposes prevail. We *will* be the church that God intended from eternity past. That's good news!

So let's persevere and continue the march toward true biblical reconciliation in the church. In the words of an old spiritual, "God don't want no coward soldiers." These words remind us that a soldier must be brave, must be courageous—because we are in a battle. We'll be talking about that in our last chapter. The time is urgent. We've lost a lot of ground for the kingdom because we were asleep on this crucial issue. But we must fight while it is still day. And, I don't know about you, but I'm not tired yet. And I'm not giving up on what God has called me to do.

Let's encourage our hearts by these powerful words from Scripture:

Galatians 6:9—Let us not lose heart in doing good, for in due time we will reap if we do not grow weary.

2 Thessalonians 3:13—But as for you, brethren, do not grow weary of doing good.

James 1:12—Blessed is a man who perseveres under trial; for once he has been approved, he will receive the crown of life which the Lord has promised to those who love Him.

PRAYER · Oh Lord, how we need You to help us to remain committed to Your call on our lives to be reconciled to one another. Help us, Lord, to not become discouraged when there are few who care enough to fight for oneness in Your church. Help us to push through the naysayers and those who fight against a united church. Help us to set our eyes on Your finished work and to trust You to use us for Your glory—until Jesus comes. In His name, Amen.

PRAYER, THE WEAPON OF OUR WARFARE

I find then the principle that evil is present in me, the one who wants to do good. For I joyfully concur with the law of God in the inner man, but I see a different law in the members of my body, waging war against the law of my mind and making me a prisoner of the law of sin which is in my members. —ROMANS 7:21-23

Finally, be strong in the Lord and in the strength of His might. Put on the full armor of God, so that you will be able to stand firm against the schemes of the devil. —EPHESIANS 6:10-11

We've talked about God's great vision for His church: biblical reconciliation. By His great mercy and the gift to us of His undeserved grace, He reconciled us to Himself and then called each of us to the ministry of reconciliation. His grand vision is for each of us to be so motivated by His love that we make it our mission to be one with every other believer in Jesus Christ. By this great love unbelievers will be drawn to Him.

We've discussed the important steps that we must take to

get there. We must accept that there is only one race—one blood. We must lament the brokenness of our past. We must make mutual confessions and forgive one another. We must repent and remain committed to this great work. But there is one more thing that is required, and it is the foundation for everything else. And that is prayer. Without it nothing God-honoring happens.

The devil believes God's Word. I wish we did.

It's like the story of the pastor who was taking a group of young men on a tour of his huge church complex. He showed them the enormous sanctuary, the impressive office wing, and the corridor of unending classrooms. But he slowed down when he came to a small room in the lower level of the building. Before opening the door he said, "This is the power source for all that we do here." Inside that room were five mothers of the church—praying.

What the apostle Paul talks about in Romans and in Ephesians is that whenever the believer tries to do good—that which pleases the Lord—there is a war within. The Enemy has been hard at work since the beginning of time to say that God's way does not work. He began his destruction in the garden of Eden with Adam and Eve by calling the truth of God's Word into question: "Indeed, has God said, 'You shall not eat from any tree of the garden'?" (Gen. 3:1b). And he continued by casting doubt on God's good intentions: "You surely will not die! For God knows that in the day you eat from it your eyes will be opened, and you will be like God, knowing good and evil" (vv. 4–5).

Since the beginning of time Satan has not changed his approach. He hasn't changed anything. He hasn't needed to. The poison that he used in the garden still works today. We've each felt his fiery darts—the darts of prejudice, discouragement, apathy, complacency. And we can certainly see how his darts have crippled the church. There's more working against the church coming together across ethnic and cultural lines than just our personal prejudices. The Enemy has staked his claim on keeping us divided and keeping us from trusting one another. He knows that what Jesus said before He went to Calvary was true, that if we are one—the world will believe! The devil believes God's Word. I wish we did.

He has launched a fierce attack: "For our struggle is not against flesh and blood, but against the rulers, against the powers, against the world forces of this darkness, against the spiritual forces of wickedness in the heavenly places" (Eph. 6:12).

Some people don't believe we should talk about the devil. They think that by talking about him we give him more power than he deserves. I don't think it makes sense to go into a battle and not know who you're fighting against. And if you're in a battle and don't even know there's a battle going on, you're going to be wiped out. This thing of reconciliation is one of the devil's main battlegrounds. We need to know that in order to be ready to fight well.

In our own strength we are no match for the Enemy. But with God on our side, we stand like David did against Goliath.

"You come to me with a sword, a spear, and a javelin, but I come to you in the name of the LORD of hosts, the God of the armies of Israel, whom you have taunted. This day the LORD will deliver you up into my hands, and I will strike

you down and remove your head from you. And I will give the dead bodies of the army of the Philistines this day to the birds of the sky and the wild beasts of the earth, that all the earth may know that there is a God in Israel, and that all this assembly may know that the LORD does not deliver by sword or by spear; for the battle is the LORD's and He will give you into our hands." (1 Sam. 17:45–47)

In this battle for biblical reconciliation, we don't go against the Enemy with swords, spears, and javelins. We don't fight with small stones and slingshots. We pray. We pray. We pray because this battle is the Lord's. And by praying we call down the whole army of God to defeat the enemies of reconciliation. Like David, we believe that God's power is more than enough to bring victory.

Some people think that those of us who believe in social justice don't believe in prayer, that we don't pray enough. They think that because they don't really understand what prayer is. They think it's something that you do at a set time; that it's just asking God for what you want. But prayer is more than that. Prayer is listening for God's answer. It's that intimate practice of asking according to His will and moving as He directs. I love the words of this song, "Lead me, guide me, along the way. For if you lead me, I cannot stray. Lord, let me walk each day with thee. Lead me, O Lord, lead me." That's what prayer is.

And I'm convinced that prayer and work go together. We've got to work and we've got to pray. We've got to do all that we can humanly do to move toward God's vision for unity in the body of Christ. And we've got to pray that He will reign over our efforts and will bring His supernatural power to bear against the forces that oppose us.

The old saints used to say, "I've got a telephone in my bosom and I can call him up anytime." And they would sing, "Just a Little Talk with Jesus" (written by Cleavant Derricks):

> *Now let us have a little talk with Jesus*
> *And we'll tell him all about our troubles*
> *He will hear our faintest cry*
> *And he will answer by and by*
> *Feel the little prayer wheel turning*
> *And you'll know that the fire is burning*
> *Just a little talk with Jesus makes it right.*

They believed that God could fix their problems. They believed that God listened to their prayers. And they were confident that He would answer "by and by." Those who were slaves would have to steal away in secret meeting places in the "brush harbors" to pray. If they were discovered, they could be beaten. But "the prayer meetings served as such an important part of slaves' religious experience that they were willing to risk physical harm in order to worship."[1]

Those who have fought for reconciliation have believed the same thing. This is how Martin Luther King Jr. prayed:

> *O God . . . we thank Thee for the lives of great saints and*
> *prophets in the past, who have revealed to us that we can stand*
> *up amid the problems and difficulties and trials of life and*
> *not give in. We thank Thee for our foreparents, who've given*
> *us something in the midst of the darkness of exploitation and*
> *oppression to keep going. And grant that we will go on with the*
> *proper faith and the proper determination of will, so that we*
> *will be able to make a creative contribution to this world and in*
> *our lives. In the name and spirit of Jesus we pray.*[2]

Another soldier for reconciliation was Mary McLeod Bethune. She was born into a family of seventeen children, and was the daughter of former slaves. I was moved when I read her prayer about justice and diversity:

> *Father, we call Thee Father because we love Thee. We are glad to be called Thy children, and to dedicate our lives to the service that extends through willing hearts and hands to the betterment of all mankind. We send a cry of Thanksgiving for people of all races, creeds, classes, and colors the world over, and pray that through the instrumentality of our lives the spirit of peace, joy, fellowship, and brotherhood shall circle the world. We know that this world is filled with discordant notes, but help us, Father, to so unite our efforts that we may all join in one harmonious symphony for peace and brotherhood, justice, and equality of opportunity for all men. The tasks performed today with forgiveness for all our errors, we dedicate, dear Lord, to Thee. Grant us strength and courage and faith and humility sufficient for the tasks assigned to us.*[3]

It will take nothing less than God's mountain-moving power to bring us together as one.

Yes, we believe in prayer. We believe in God's power to change things . . . and we believe in His power to change us. Here's where we can start in our praying.

• **Pray for His will to be done.** The prayer that Jesus taught His disciples encouraged them to pray that His will would be done on earth as it is in heaven. We know what

His will is for reconciliation within the church. His prayer in John 17 made it clear that His heart's desire is that we are one just as He and the Father are one. His will is for one Church that crosses ethnic, cultural, and class lines and is focused on bringing Him glory until He returns to redeem His bride. This picture of the church is what must fuel our prayers.

We've got to ask Him to move everything that stands in the way of His will being accomplished. This is a big ask. In light of how divided the church is today, only God and His power will make this happen. Jesus taught, saying, " . . . for truly I say to you, if you have faith the size of a mustard seed, you will say to this mountain, 'Move from here to there,' and it will move; and nothing will be impossible to you" (Matt. 17:20).

We serve a mountain-moving God! It will take nothing less than His mountain-moving power to bring us together as one. We must ask Him, believing that He can accomplish this great task. I've heard it said that we should regularly pray prayers that are so big that only God could accomplish them. I believe that. And we shouldn't be afraid to ask God to do the impossible, because we know His record. He's not afraid of the impossible, from opening the Red Sea to raising Lazarus from the dead. All impossible deeds. But He did it. And He can make us one together. He can turn our hearts to one another. He can do it!

• **Pray for our hearts.** After we pray for His will to be done, we need to pray for our own hearts. David said, "Create in me a clean heart, O God, and renew a steadfast spirit within me" (Ps. 51:10). In the words of an old spiritual, "It's me, it's me, it's me, oh Lord. Standing in the need of prayer."

If ever we need the Lord to heal our hearts, it's in this area of reconciliation. We all struggle with what Paul talked about in Romans 7. Even when we know the good that we should do,

---

*When we are fearful, our prayers are probably more powerful,
because they're probably more honest.*

---

we are more likely to do the evil. There is a war going on in our
own being. We are often motivated by selfish pride and a desire
to look out for ourselves. We need for our hearts to be broken
over the lack of reconciliation in the body of Christ. And we
need for God to give us His heart for the other. We need for our
eyes to be opened to the truth that we are all one blood.

After He changes our hearts we need Him to move us beyond our fears and anxieties into loving relationship with one
another. When we are fearful, our prayers are probably more
powerful . . . because they're probably more honest. We need
Him to help us lay aside our prejudices and wrong-headed
notions about one another and help us to learn from and with
one another. We need His help to be honest and transparent
with one another, to grieve our past and be ready to move
forward together as one.

• **Pray for our brothers and sisters.** In addition to praying for His will to be done and our own hearts to be changed,
we are challenged to pray for our brothers and sisters—those
who look like us and those who don't look like us. Pray for
broken hearts and changed minds.

William Pannell said in one of his sermons that the ugliest
four-letter word in the English vocabulary is *them*.[4] It's a word
that separates and divides. It's important that we know their
names. It's really hard to dislike someone you pray for regularly. One of the most important things we can do to move
the cause of reconciliation forward is to pray for the brothers

and sisters who we have been separate from. "You have heard that it was said, 'You shall love your neighbor and hate your enemy.' But I say to you, love your enemies and pray for those who persecute you, so that you may be sons of your Father who is in heaven; for He causes His sun to rise on the evil and the good, and sends rain on the righteous and the unrighteous" (Matt. 5:43–45).

We can pray for God's blessing on those we have felt separated from and for their hearts to be softened even as ours are. We can pray for opportunities to engage with them in new ways and for a new spirit of fellowship and brotherhood to develop. We can pray that they will not become discouraged if their first try at reaching out does not work. We will all need the Lord to keep us moving forward and to not give up when we are rejected and things don't go the way we want them to.

• **Pray for organizations that are fighting for reconciliation.** We can pray mightily for organizations that are fighting to bring us together as one. When we worked together with Wayne Gordon to organize the Christian Community Development Association (CCDA) in 1989 we had no idea where God would lead us. But it has been a labor of love. The organization has been tirelessly committed to God's effort to restore people to right relationship with Himself and to their families and communities. This work has continued alongside countless other like-minded organizations.

We need to pray for CCDA, the Mendenhall Ministries, Voice of Calvary in Jackson, Mississippi, the Harambee Christian Family Center in Pasadena, California, and the John and Vera Mae Perkins Foundation, as well as other organizations across this country that have labored long and hard for reconciliation and justice.

As I near the end of my own life, I'm aware of how much we need the Lord to sustain the work that bears our name. As I hand this work off to my successors, I pray that they will not become weary in the challenges that lie ahead. Our organization and countless others have been carried forward by men and women who love the Lord and love one another. My prayer is that the work will continue as unto the Lord and until He says, "well done."

• **Pray for the Church.** And finally we need to pray for the church. We can pray for the leadership of our local churches to sense God's call for oneness. We can ask God to bring revival to His church. We need the kind of revival that convicts us of our past sins of prejudice and racism. We need the kind of revival that changes how the church looks and how denominations work together to accomplish His purposes.

We can pray especially for the rise of more and more multicultural churches across this land. We should ask the Lord to help those church leaders remain encouraged and not give up in the face of difficulties from without and within. Throughout this book we have sprinkled the stories of four multicultural churches that have been intentional about applying Scripture to their life and practice. The roads they took to becoming multicultural are different from one another and reflect the creativity of our Lord. Pray for each of them to remain faithful to their prototype and calling.

We can pray that we will all get a glimpse of what He can do if we are fully committed to the vision of oneness. We can pray for a zeal to do His bidding, and to be a model of Christ's character before this watching world.

In his book *Kingdom Prayer*, Tony Evans talks about a prayer crusade in Columbia, South Carolina, that was centered around reconciliation and community restoration. They were expecting around 25,000 people to attend, half black and half white. But there was a problem. A thunderstorm was making its way in their direction and threatening to prevent the whole event from taking place. The pastors and leaders of the event met to pray and ask God to turn the storm back. For some reason their prayers seemed empty and almost powerless. But a little lady named Linda asked if she could pray. Her prayer was powerful as she reminded the Lord that His name was at stake. She literally called the powers of heaven to come to their aid.

As 25,000 people watched, the storm advanced quickly in their direction. A lot of people began putting up umbrellas, but Linda didn't move. She sat and waited to see how the Lord would move. And then this happened:

> *The rain rushed toward the stadium like a wall of water. Yet when it hit the stadium, the path of the pounding rain split. Half of the rain went on one side of the stadium. The other half went on the other side. And then it literally met on the far side of the stadium. All the while, Linda sat there with a confident look on her face.*[5]

That night 25,000 people watched a miracle take place. They saw God's power affirming His heart for the work of reconciliation and they saw His power accessed through the believing prayer of a little lady named Linda.

I'm thinking that we need some sisters (and brothers) like Linda who will storm heaven with believing prayer. We can ask, knowing that His heart is bent toward our efforts to become one. We can pray believing. And we can believe in our prayers because we already know God's will for the Church to be one.

PRAYER · Oh God of heaven. We remember Your great deeds for Your people. You created the world with Your Word. You spoke and it was so. You called Abraham and made of him a great nation. You delivered that nation out of slavery in Egypt and took them into the Promised Land. You kept Your Word even though Your people rebelled. You brought a Savior through their lineage. You allowed Your dear Son to die for the sins of the world; and You left Your church to carry on Your witness to the world. There is nothing too hard for You. Oh, how we need You, Lord. How we need Your Spirit to awaken us and make us one. As the first-century saints prayed, Lord, we ask the same—that You would send your healing power to make us one. One in purpose. One in spirit. One in love. Until You come again. Amen.

LIVING IT OUT

Epiphany Fellowship

LEAD PASTOR: Dr. Eric Mason

PHILADELPHIA, PA

ACTS 29 CHURCH, AFFILIATED WITH THE SOUTHERN BAPTIST CONVENTION

We sensed a call to plant five years before we hit our context. I began praying and writing out a general—yet urban and contextual—vision. I read everything I could on the subject. I read everything I could get my hands on that had to do with church planting—especially in an urban context.

The pre-planting process was quite intense. I took on a residency in a different context than I was used to. That church planting residency provided the incubation time for my wife and I to get what was needed for us to go and serve our city.

Once we got on the ground, we did tons of prayer walks and neighborhood interviews. We went everywhere: from the college campuses, projects, subways, and main streets. We found ourselves drowned in Philadelphia as we were falling in love with the people and culture of the city. We ate the food (a lot of it) and built relationships with people no matter their color or background. We started a Bible study and leadership development time. During this time we were raising funding. As we began to advertise and develop a web presence, people began to swarm into this gospel project. People moved from as far away as Dallas, Texas, and LA to be a part. We met in a small row house for about six months and we outgrew it. We did outreach to our target area. The largest outreach brought about two thousand people during the course of the day as we shared the gospel, fed the city, and shared Jesus through music and evangelism. The next day we launched. God has been good.

Our church was officially organized in September 17, 2006. The area was in the process of gentrification and was a perfect setting for the ministry. The setting was multicultural and there were deep concerns within each group that needed attention. Being faithful to the gospel required us to be faithful to the people God called us to engage.

Colossians 1:28 talks about admonishing and teaching every man that they may be presented complete in Christ. We felt God's call to engage each of the groups within the context of Epiphany. Our heart was for Epiphany to reflect the neighborhood where we are located. There were the urban poor, most of whom were African American. There were professionals, both black and white, who had moved back into the neighborhood, who we would challenge to lovingly engage the poor. And there were college students we would have the privilege to teach and inspire to become missional. We were grateful for this unique blend of groups to do ministry with.

Our core values and mission statement are built around the themes of Christ-Centeredness, Commitment, Community, Conversions, and Culturally Relevant Ministry. In our multiethnic context it is crucial that we contextualize our ministry without violating the truth of Scripture. We believe that Titus 1:5 calls for a plurality of elders and Acts 15 teaches that the leader should be a first among equals who functions as the directional communicator within the leadership structure. This shared leadership of the collective builds in account-ability. We have found that millennials tend to be suspicious of leadership, so this shared style builds trust and greater accountability. Because we are a multiethnic church our eldership is multiethnic.

Our deaconship ministry is not a board but is a community of servants. We were challenged to make sure that our organizational model aligned closely with Scripture (Acts 6; 1 Tim. 3:8–11). Multiethnic millennials see a difference between the Bible and the structures in the church. Many of them came from churches where the senior pastor and deacons have an adversarial relationship. Our desire was to return to a more biblical model that removes bureaucracy from the equation. Our deacons are representative of our multiethnic congregation. They lead ministries and teach in microspheres and lead discipleship.

We believe that music is a valuable tool to communicate biblical truth and to connect with different cultures. We fuse jazz, soul, neo-soul, hip-hop, gospel, and contemporary Christian music to help speak in the cultural voices of different ethnicities. At the same time, we ensure that the rich gospel content focuses on Jesus. We balance repetition and dense wording to help our members engage on differing heart levels.

We envision the gospel taking root in the lives of the unreached people groups of North Philadelphia. And we are called to build a solid community of people who live out the good news about Jesus Christ through both life and lips. We're excited about people of different ethnicities submitting to the Lord Jesus Christ and in turn becoming indigenous missionaries globally. We are a church-planting church and have planted multiethnic churches in Los Angeles; Brooklyn; Camden; Germantown (Philadelphia); Baltimore; Wilmington; Delaware; and Gloucester City, New Jersey.

While the universal church is multiethnic, by and large the local church is not. The church should reflect the context that it is in. Therefore, just as in Antioch, the church engaged those with the gospel who were in their sphere. If the surrounding area is multiethnic, the church should be on some level. Multiethnic churches aren't to be pressed on churches that are in homogenous settings. For those churches that are in homogenous settings, they should work hard to grow their racial IQ. They should become culturally literate and aware so that if other ethnicities visit or move into their neighborhood they are prepared.

THE GREATEST OF THESE IS LOVE

But now faith, hope, love, abide these three; but the greatest of these is love. —1 CORINTHIANS 13:13

Yes, it's going to take prayer, commitment, repentance, forgiveness, confession, lament, a clear vision for oneness—but can I tell you what the greatest motivator is for getting this done? It's the love of Jesus. When I think about the fact that He loved me, even though I grew up on the wrong side of the tracks, in a bootlegging family, and even though I lived for twenty-six years without thinking much of Him . . . I am overwhelmed by His love.

The love of Christ and His example of suffering has strengthened me over the years. Something about His being willing to die on the cross for me, in spite of my sin and my unworthiness. And the idea of Him forgiving the very ones who were killing Him and praying for them while they were doing it . . . well, if you think about that long enough, it will change you. It will force you to get outside yourself and ask if you are willing to love others the same way.

Most of what I will share in this final chapter is very personal. I want to provide a window into my heart and into some very special relationships that have fueled my zeal for reconciliation. My hope is that what you read will show you how you can get started in earnest helping to make His vision of oneness real for the Church today.

I wish I could say I have walked the straight and narrow ever since I accepted Him into my heart at the age of twenty-seven, but I've had stumbles and falls. I've wanted to hold up the banner for social justice and for reconciliation, but there have been moments when my arms have been weakened. There have been seasons of despair and difficulty. But I have clung to His love and it has kept me. There will be valleys and stumbles along your journey if you engage this battle for reconciliation, but His love will keep you.

One of my deepest struggles has been keeping my love for this great work balanced alongside the love for my family. I'm afraid that there have been times when my family suffered because of the lack of balance. That has been my one regret. I cannot change what is past, but I can encourage those who will take up the mantle to remember to keep first things first. We give all we can and trust that love will cover a multitude of sins.

His love has done that for me. It has covered my human responses to the hurts of this life. It has encouraged me when I wondered whether the sacrifices were worth it all. It has soothed my heart when it was burdened with the weight of anger and betrayal. What kind of love is this that would love us even when we fall? I should have been dead a long time ago! Why wasn't I? My son Spencer used to say that God had a guardian angel on me every day, and at night He'd have to put a new angel on me because the first one was worn out. His love has protected me. And it has filled me to overflowing with a joy that I cannot describe. Oh, the joy of His love!

The word for this kind of sacrificial love is *agape*: "Unconditional love that is always giving and impossible to take or be a taker. It devotes total commitment to seek your highest best no matter how anyone may respond. This form of love is totally selfless and does not change whether the love given is returned or not."[1]

I don't think there's a more beautiful story of this kind of love between brothers in the Bible than the relationship between David and Jonathan. What an unlikely friendship, a prince and a lowly shepherd boy. But God in His providence brought both of them together to cement a bond of true friendship and love.

"Now it came about when he had finished speaking to Saul, that the soul of Jonathan was knit to the soul of David, and Jonathan loved him as himself. . . . Then Jonathan made a covenant with David because he loved him as himself. Jonathan stripped himself of the robe that was on him and gave it to David, with his armor, including his sword and his bow and his belt" (1 Sam. 18:1, 3-4).

I looked at one of my white brothers and said, "Man, I don't think I could love nobody any more than I love you!"

In *Leap Over a Wall*, Eugene Peterson says, "Friendship with David complicated Jonathan's life enormously. He risked losing his father's favor and willingly sacrificed his own royal future. But neither the risk nor the loss deterred him; he became and stayed David's friend."[2] That's true biblical love. And I believe this is how God wants every believer to feel toward all believers, whether black or white. This sacrificial love was the driving force of Jesus' life and ministry, and it still is today. Without it we will never accomplish the work of reconciliation. We simply cannot do it without understanding that His love compels us to love our enemies. There's an African proverb that I think expresses beautifully just how important this face-to-face kind of friendship is: "When I saw you from afar, I thought you were a monster. When you got closer, I thought you were just an animal. When you got even closer, I saw that you were a human, but when we were face to face I realized that you were my brother."

The closer we get to one another the easier it will be for the fear to go away. We'll see that we have so much more in common than we ever thought. And the door will be opened for us to love one another with true biblical love.

I have been blessed with this kind of love from my family and many brothers and sisters in Christ, both black and white. A special group of brothers gather every Tuesday for Bible study at our center. We meet at 5:30 in the morning and have been doing this for years. I was overwhelmed by how much love we have for one another. I looked at one of my white brothers and said, "Man, I don't think I could love nobody any more than I love you!" Another one of the brothers said, "It looks like I've opened up a well in my heart!" That's what happens when we love like Jesus did. It's like a well that rises up in your heart and overflows. It's pure joy!

God has showered His love on me by giving me so many brothers, some black and some white, that I can truly say love me. Growing up without a mother, without a father, and then losing my brother left me at a deficit of love. I seek it desperately. That kind of a deficit can be painful. Most of my friends did not have a brother or if they had a brother there was some deficiency in their relationship. I have become the brother they needed; they have become the brothers I needed.

———

I really believe that we give to others what we long for.

———

Henri Nouwen said this: "The greatest gift my friendship can give to you is the gift of your Belovedness. I can give that gift only insofar as I have claimed it for myself. Isn't that what friendship is all about: giving to each other the gift of our Belovedness . . . there is that voice . . . that whispers softly or declares loudly: 'You are my Beloved, on you my favor rests.' It is certainly not easy to hear that voice in a world filled with voices that shout: 'You are no good, you are ugly; you are worthless, you are despicable, you are nobody—unless you can demonstrate the opposite.' These voices are so loud and so persistent that it is easy to believe them. That's the great trap. It is the trap of self-rejection."[3]

I wish people could see that we get from others what we give. Jesus said, "In everything, therefore, treat people the same way you want them to treat you, for this is the Law and the Prophets" (Matt. 7:12). If we treat people how we want to be treated, God will bless us. I really believe that we give to others what we long for. And if you have that deep long- ing to be loved, it's sort of a pain in your heart. I don't know . . . maybe we hurt and hate others out of that pain if it isn't tended to. My weakness and my strength have been in my over competitive nature. I've tried to out-love my friends. I find myself competing out of my loneliness to love my friends more than they love me. But they always win.

My heart aches when I remember my father walking away from me when I was a small child. I think that's why I can't stand to break off relationships, even when people try to poison my mind against a person because they don't like them. I can't quit on my friends. Every potential friend can become a better friend if I don't give up.

The truth is that most of my friends became friends around some type of disagreement. There's probably no topic that is more open to disagreement than that of reconciliation. But for me this has provided opportunity for discussion and negotiation. It's in that negotiation that we become friends. I say, "We may say things different, but basically we believe the same thing." And another friendship is born.

One of those very special friend relationships has been with Wayne Gordon. Wayne and I talk on the telephone almost every day of the week now. In the beginning we would talk about three times a week, but more recently it's been every day. We decided that we need to talk and pray for each other every day. We've been doing life together like this for more than thirty years now. We decided a long time ago that we were going to link arms together—one black brother and one white brother—and we would see where God would take us.

We met after Wayne heard me speak at Wheaton College almost forty-five years ago. He called and asked if I would visit him. He picked me up from the airport and brought me to his center. He was already friends with Tom Skinner and had a deep passion for reconciliation. So there was already a foundation there for a friendship to grow on. Our friendship has been so rich and has enhanced my life. It has given me a desire to make other friends that would draw that same love out of me.

Our friendship has been pretty much a constant ever since it began. We didn't have time to get mad and stay mad with each other. Both of our wives could look at us and let us know if we were off base. We became leaders and organizers together of the Christian Community Development Association (CCDA) because we were inseparable. People could not get between us. Wayne is a super-manager and I am a super-idealist and a super-principle guy, with very little management skill. One of us had the philosophy and the other had the management. I knew how to love people; he knew how to manage people.

When I think about what made our love grow more and more, it was that whenever we were together we were competing to love the other more. When my son died, Wayne stopped what he was doing and came to spend Friday, Saturday, and Sunday with me. He was there to walk through that valley with me. He has allowed his children to become friends and grandchildren to me.

At a recent CCDA conference we were talking about fundraising. Most of the people thought that all the donors were my friends. But they were actually Wayne's friends first. He had caused his friends to become my friends. And I think this is the secret to how we can win this fight for reconciliation. If each one would reach across to the other and merge their circles of influence. If we could do this as individual Christians and as churches God could do great things with us.

I have been enriched, blessed, and comforted by the true wealth of friendship. If I were to begin naming all the names of these special people, there would not be enough room to contain them. So richly has God blessed me with men like Wayne, both black and white, who have stood by my side and held my arms up in the places of weakness and rejoiced with me in times of celebration. If I had known the true power this friendship afforded me, I would have been more courageous along the way.

When it's all said and done, love is a choice. It's a decision. I choose the way of love. I've chosen to be marked by it. What I have reaped in return has been joy unspeakable.

What I wish for you almost more than anything else is that each one would choose love. And then that each one could find their own Wayne, a brother or sister or church from the other side to do this life with. It makes the journey so much sweeter. Link arms with your Wayne and see what the Lord will do for the cause of reconciliation.

Peter Scholtes penned the words to "They'll Know We are Christians by Our Love" in 1968, inspired by the words of John 13:35: "By this all men will know that you are My disciples, if you have love for one another." The title of the hymn originated from a phrase that non-believers used to describe Christian believers in the early Church: "Behold, how they love one another!"[4]

What would it take for unbelievers to say this again? What would it take for them to marvel at how deep our love is for one another? Nothing less than the sacrificial love of God on display again and again as we choose to die to ourselves and bury our age-old excuses for remaining in separate camps. It will require the church to rise up to our calling to glorify our God by crucifying the old man and living anew as One . . . One Church . . . One Blood.

> Love never fails; but if there are gifts of prophecy, they will be done away; if there are tongues, they will cease; if there is knowledge, it will be done away. For we know in part and

we prophesy in part; but when the perfect comes, the partial will be done away. When I was a child, I used to speak like a child, think like a child, reason like a child; when I became a man, I did away with childish things. For now we see in a mirror dimly, but then face to face; now I know in part, but then I will know fully just as I also have been fully known. But now faith, hope, love, abide these three; but the greatest of these is love. —1 CORINTHIANS 13:8-13

Now the God of peace, who brought up from the dead the great Shepherd of the sheep through the blood of the eternal covenant, even Jesus our Lord, equip you in every good thing to do His will, working in us that which is pleasing in His sight, through Jesus Christ, to whom be the glory forever and ever. Amen. —HEBREWS 13:20-21

PRAYER · Lord Jesus, teach us what it means to love like You love. Cause us to become uncomfortable with surface-level friendships. Help us to yearn and hunger for deep fellowship that is real and can be seen and that will light the way for those who are in darkness. Would You set ablaze in our hearts a passion for You, for all of Your people, and for Your church. Lord, make us One. Make us rejoice when the other rejoices. Make us weep when the other weeps. Lord, make us One. For Your glory, Amen.

EPILOGUE:
ALMOST HOME

Well . . . I've had my say. I believe that if we can get it into our heads and our hearts that we are one, we will make it. We are one human race. We are one blood, all created from one man, Adam. And we are saved by one blood—the blood of Jesus, the Son of God who gave His life to reconcile us to the Father—and to one another.

Blood carries with it the idea of life, because life is in the blood. But it also carries the idea of suffering. It's this concept of suffering that I'm most aware of now. Not just suffering for the sake of suffering, but suffering coupled with joy. If we're going to make the kind of progress that we need to make with reconciliation, we have got to be willing to suffer. And we've got to be able to see joy as the end product of our suffering.

God calls us to be willing to suffer for His purposes. Jesus was the perfect model of a Suffering Servant: "Who for the joy set before Him endured the cross, despising the shame, and has sat down at the right hand of the throne of God" (Heb. 12:2). We've got to see suffering as a virtue and be willing to stay in the struggle until the Lord calls us home. That's what made the heroes of the fight for reconciliation so special. Every one of them fought until their day was done. Those who are still alive are continuing to fight this battle for biblical reconciliation. Quitting is not an option.

As I write this and observe what is happening in our nation, with groups taking to the streets in Charlottesville, Virginia, I am gravely concerned. Our people were damaged greatly by our years of captivity as slaves, but there was something about that experience that allowed us to accept pain— to suffer as Jesus did. And by the grace of God we were able to forgive and love our oppressors. We went to war and fought right alongside white folks. We fought for freedom and did not become haters of our nation, even though it did not live up to its promise. And when we began to make progress we did not become terrorists. We did not take up arms and kill those who had oppressed us. We wanted to move forward. We wanted to make a difference. In spite of everything that had happened we still had hope.

My good friend Milton Smith said, "For me one of the greatest gifts that our black brothers and sisters have given to us is in always remaining hopeful. Your hope in God has been a gift to us as white Americans and to this country."

During the Civil Rights era, Martin Luther King Jr. worked hard to train leaders who helped prepare young people to stand in front of police officers with dogs, billy clubs, fire hoses, and on horseback and not fight back. We learned that the power of God was great enough to show us how to suffer well. We trusted Him to make it right. And He began to move on our behalf in ways that we never could if we had taken up arms to fight.

I'm afraid of this violence that is breaking out on our streets. Hate groups have always existed in our country. That's nothing new. But we have never allowed ourselves to fall to that place of revenge and fighting back. I am praying to the

Lord that our young people who desperately want equality, dignity, and respect do not become terrorists. Violence gives birth to more violence. Hate births more hate. We cannot allow this. The advances that we have made in this country did not come because we took to the streets to fight. We need to remind ourselves that God fights for those who trust His purposes. We are to be marked by love, truth, and forgiveness. His commands to love our enemies and to turn the other cheek are as real today as they were when first spoken. As James says, we "must be quick to hear, slow to speak and slow to anger" (James 1:19).

We have the moral advantage and the moral high road when we refuse to fight. Our ancestors knew this great truth. They suffered well. Their suffering was undergirded with the joy of the Lord. They rested in the assurance that He would deliver them—if not in this life, certainly in the next.

But we have to overcome our fears. Fear will immobilize us or cause us to do things that are ungodly. It's only natural to be afraid of what will happen if we don't fight back. We were afraid in the '60s and '70s in the South. We were very afraid. But our fears made our prayers more powerful, more honest. "God we need You! Lord, help us!" God uses the person who does what He says in the midst of fear. Courage is born in the face of fear.

As I've had opportunity to counsel with pastors and students at the University of Virginia in Charlottttesville, my message to them has been this: "Real commitment is doing things that you don't like to do in the face of fear." We are at a pivotal moment in history, and the things that are happening now reveal how much work is left to be done. This struggle for reconciliation is not going to be won in the streets. It's going to be won by believers in Jesus Christ who choose to live out the truth of the gospel. It's going to be won in the hearts and minds of men, women, boys, and girls who choose to believe that our 99.9 percent oneness trumps our .1 percent differences. It's going to be won by those who will be courageous enough to stand and tell the truth about the ugliness of ethnic hatred and the beauty of true Christian brotherhood.

In a recent interview of a young man who used to be a skinhead, he described what caused him to mend his ways. He explained that kindness, forgiveness, and compassion were like kryptonite to him. Violence charged him up. He was energized by it. But what finally wore him down was when he had a Jewish supervisor at work who was kind to him. It was when he had a black coworker who was compassionate toward him. Their compassion and kindness broke through the hard barrier of racial hate and bigotry.[1]

The Church must speak out with one voice against bigotry and racism. We have been too quiet. The time is now. A platform has been placed in front of us and we must speak with clarity and truth. We've made a mess of things, but there is a path forward. It will require us to hold fast to his vision for one Church and the biblical truth of one race. We need to lament our broken past and be willing to make some personal confessions about our own part in this mess. Then we'll have to be willing to forgive and move toward true repentance. We must be committed to the fight until the battle for reconciliation is won. And we must never forget that our power is not in guns, weapons, or armies. Our power is on our knees before our God.

> *"If. . . My people, who are called by My name humble themselves and pray and seek My face and turn from their wicked*

ways, then I will hear from heaven, will forgive their sin and will heal their land." (2 Chron. 7:13–14)

God has been stirring the hearts of denominational leaders across the country over the last several years. It should be no surprise that when God begins to stir hearts that the Enemy begins to rise up and cause more anger and strife. We must be vigilant and keep our eyes focused on our goal. We cannot afford to lose ground that has been gained. This is much too important.

I'm grateful for the next generation of fighters for biblical reconciliation. They are bold. They are brave. They have caught the vision and they are planting multicultural churches across this country. You've read their stories throughout this book. Their churches have all become multicultural communities, but the paths they took were not the same. I am encouraged by that. God is creative in how He draws His people together. I believe God will use them to ignite a flame that blazes in the heart of the church for oneness. My prayer is for God to hasten the day when every church in America is a multicultural church. Churches that are located in communities where there are no minorities can still work to increase their understanding of other ethnic groups. They can prepare their hearts so that minorities would feel comfortable visiting.

It won't happen in my lifetime, but I can see it coming. When it does, I will be among that great cloud of witnesses around the throne of God. I will mingle my voice with the voices of Wilberforce, King Jr., Skinner, and a multitude of others shouting, "Hallelujah! His kingdom is coming on earth as it is in heaven!" That will be a glorious day!

Until then, every one of us has a crucial part to play in this story of reconciliation. I know what my part is. I will preach the message of biblical reconciliation until He calls me home. I will stand on the wall to encourage and remind others that this great work is not in vain. I will tell the story until my last dying breath. That's my part. What is your part? What is it that God has specially gifted you to do in this battle for biblical reconciliation? Whatever it is, I beg you to do it as unto God until your last day.

My physical body is getting tired. I imagine this may be how the apostle Paul felt when he said, "For I am already being poured out as a drink offering, and the time of my departure has come" (2 Tim. 4:6). I feel like that on a lot of days. And it's at these times that I reflect on what it will be like to see my mother. A lot of people say that she was a "Fannie Lou Hamer" type of woman. My mother would challenge the plantation owners if they were unfair. She died because her body was too weak to nurse me, a seven-month-old baby. She died that I might live. I look forward to crossing the threshold of heaven and rushing into her arms. I'll tell her that I picked up the mantle of reconciliation and ran hard until my day was done. I want to know that she is proud of me. I want to hear her say, "You did well, son." Then I'll go looking for my two sons, Spencer and Wayne. It's going to be some kind of reunion. That "great camp meeting in the sky" . . . where we'll see Jesus and touch the face of God.

Yes, my steps are a little slower now . . . but my spirit is energized. I still have joy. I am full of hope for the future. We will get there. We will get there—together. We will get there—as one.

"When we all get to heaven,
    what a day of rejoicing that will be!
When we all see Jesus,
    we'll sing and shout the victory!"

AFTERWORD

My friends, I am writing this afterword not because I feel worthy of the honor, but because my friend asked me to. Quite frankly, I feel a bit reluctant to say a word in his shadow, questioning what could I possibly add to the words of a man who lived through so much, who loved through so much? You too might be rightly asking yourself, "What does the octogenarian son of a Mississippi sharecropper have in common with a California surfer who plays rock 'n' roll for a living?"

I suppose our common bond is this: love.

Dr. John M. Perkins has offered me many forms of love throughout the years: encouragement, wisdom, and even fiery warnings from time to time. I have had the humbling privilege of joining with him in his lifelong struggle to bring the gospel of peace to bear upon our nation's social injustices. Over the past decade, I've felt an overwhelming sense of affection flowing from Dr. Perkins. And yet, I know that am not unique in my experience of his kindness. The smile and warm welcome that he has shown me are a part of the easy friendship that he offers to any who would enter his world and walk alongside of him. Showing compassion for even those who would offer violence or hatred, he has lived out a love that breaks down walls, and destroys the superficial differences that divide us. It's truly hard to resist this kind of love. Where all are beloved. Where all are family. One blood.

Over the course of the past eighty-seven years, Dr. Perkins's eyes have seen their way through a lifetime of change. From the end of the Jim Crow laws, to our nation's first black president, and on through the white nationalist rally in Charlottesville a few months ago. The cynic might say, the more things change, the more things stay the same. The weeping prophet might agree: "The heart is more deceitful than anything. It is incurable—who can know it?" (Jer. 17:9 ISV). For many, these are times of despair. Times of terror. Where bad news comes to us from all sides.

There is a dark shadow upon our land. None of us are unaffected. Yes, institutional slavery may be a thing of the past, and yet our nation is still hobbling forward with the broken bones of racism and hatred. These United States of America are far from united, with the long, dark shadows of our history coming looming into view in heartbreaking, horrifying new ways. Friends, I say this with compassion and love: We are not innocent. There is blood on our hands. We and our fathers have turned a deaf ear to our neighbors. We have used the courts of law to justify our greed and bigotry. Even our churches are guilty, using Holy Scripture to justify racism, our racist practices, and slavery. Confession is our task.

The battle between the light and the darkness is nothing new. Nor are the shadows of racism and hatred an American invention. Almost two thousand years ago, James wrote: "What causes fights and quarrels among you? Don't they come from your desires that battle within you? You desire but do not have, so you kill. You covet but you cannot get what you want, so you quarrel and fight" (4:1–2 NIV). The human heart is a constant supply of hardship and horror. Yes, there's plenty of bad news these days, but where is the good news?

Where is the light? Where is the hope?

John Perkins has been a consistent reminder to me of what "gospel" means: the good news. THE GOOD NEWS! Yes! We are children of the light. We are forgiven. We are beloved. Why are we hopeful? Because there is a cure. Because there is a Savior. Because there is a salvation that rests upon a deeper reality than even the painful despair of these dark times. And ultimately, this very hope is what my friendship with John Perkins rests upon: the hope of forgiveness. The hope of transformation. Our hope is not in our nation, our songs, or our eloquence. No, our hope rests in the scars of our Savior alone. In the awareness that each of our flawed histories is forgiven with the same blood. He is patiently waiting for us, that none should perish but that all would have eternal life. The image of this compassionate and gracious Maker is found in each of us.

For hope to mean anything, it must wrestle with pain. It must face the darkest parts of humanity with compassion and truth. True hope must provide answers and healing for the deepest wounds. Otherwise it is but a Band-Aid on the broken bones of our society. A well-intentioned pleasantry that actually does more harm than good. True hope is an awareness of a reality beneath the pain. Beneath the problem.

John Perkins reminds us of a hope far below the skin. A strong, beautiful truth beneath the thin surface of racism. Under our skin-deep differences lies a weighty commonality: we are one blood. One human race. It is upon this foundation of truth that we see race and racism as human inventions. And humanity as God's creation. We are one. Yes, underneath the surface of racism there is a much stronger love binding us together: the love of Love Himself.

Someday we will enter into eternity, passing this planet on

to the next generation. I'm reminded that what we lose here on earth will be loosed in heaven. And what we bind here on earth will be bound in heaven. And I pray to the God who made this human race that we, His children, would bind our arrogance and pride. That we would let loose a flood of justice. That our children would see past the petty differences on the surface of our skin to view the image of God written in our very hearts.

We have each been handed this task not because of our ability, but because of the need. And just like the words I have attempted to put at the end of this book, we have each been given this honor in spite of our fears and inadequacies. The high privilege of loving through all barriers has been given to each of us, like an afterword to the lives of those who have gone before us. And so this book ends with the burden of a question: what will we do with the love that we have received? If John Perkins's life story is the book, what afterword will our lives write?

Dr. Perkins's life reminds me of another who showed us the way of love long ago. A marginalized man who lived on the outskirts of the empire, not given the full rights of citizenship. A man whose easy friendship was offered to any who would enter His world and walk alongside Him. A man who looked past the superficial differences, into the heart of man. A friend of even sinners like myself—a Man of Sorrows, a carpenter's son, the Light of the World, a friend who sticks closer than a brother. A man who showed me what true love looks like. And in His name I will continue to hope. I will continue to love. I will continue to fight the good fight. Not because I feel worthy of the honor, but because my friend asked me to.

—JON FOREMAN

Front man for Grammy-award-winning rock band Switchfoot

STUDY GUIDE

Introduction

1. Dr. Perkins argues that we haven't been able to fix the reconciliation problem in our country because we've been applying solutions without understanding the problem. Do you agree or disagree with this? Why or why not?

2. How would you define biblical reconciliation?

3. How engaged have you been in the cause of reconciliation?

   a. Little to none

   b. Have supported it from the sidelines

   c. Have been very engaged through events and activism.

4. What is your attitude about biblical reconciliation as you begin reading this book?

5. Do you agree that there is an urgency for the message of biblical reconciliation to be accomplished in our country? Why or why not?

Chapter One: The Church Should Look Like That

1. Why was it significant that God chose to reveal the good news of the gospel to shepherds?

2. The message of equality was heralded in our Declaration of Independence, yet many of the signers had slaves. How do we reconcile these truths?

3. How does Christ's priestly prayer in John 17 endorse the effort to make the church multicultural?

4. Explain the difficulties Peter and the first-century church had in understanding the practical application of the message of biblical reconciliation.

5. Dr. Perkins describes how coming to faith in Christ almost immediately began to change his heart toward white people. Why don't we see this happening across the church in America?

6. Discuss the process of merging a black church and a white church that Shiloh and Ridgewood experienced. What issues do you think were presented?

7. Do you agree that there is a "vision-shaped vacuum" in the Church? Why or why not?

Chapter Two: One Race, One Blood

1. What is your understanding of race?

2. What is "whiteness," and how has it figured into our ideas of race?

3. What specifically does the Bible teach about race? About ethnicity?

4. The curse of Ham extending to the curse of black people is a popular myth. When did you first hear of this myth? How do we know this is untrue?

5. Why have issues of "skin color, hair texture, language, and ethnic origin" become more important than our oneness?

6. Dr. Perkins suggests that "for reconciliation to be achieved in the church a place must be made for minorities to serve in positions of leadership." Do you agree or disagree with this? Explain your response.

Chapter Three: A Lament for Our Broken Past

1. What is lament and why is it such a lost practice among believers today?

2. If one-third of the Psalms are lament, and the Psalms were the worship songs when the people of God met, what should we understand about how crucial lament is today?

3. Why have we, as black and white Christians, been content with the truth that the 11:00 worship hour is the most segregated time in our country?

4. How was the American practice of slavery distinctly different from the biblical concept of enslavement?

5. If we believe in God's sovereignty, we must accept that He had divine purpose in allowing slavery to proceed in America. According to Tony Evans, what was God's intent?

6. What does it mean for the church to spend great resources to focus on the church in developing countries yet overlook communities in darkness in their own areas?

7. How can the display that is planned for the summer of 2018 in Montgomery, Alabama, help us along the journey to lament?

Chapter Four: The Healing Balm of Confession

1. Dr. Perkins suggests that, like the prodigal son, the Church has walked away from the standards that God set for us. What do you see as the standards that are guiding the church today?

2. How has anger on the part of blacks played a significant role in the struggle for reconciliation?

3. Explain the historical and current aspects of and implications of this anger.

4. How are you impacted by John Piper's statement on page 86?

5. Are you conscious of white privilege, or do you feel that it is a myth?

6. What are you fearful of as it relates to this discussion of biblical reconciliation?

7. Do you have a personal confession that you feel led to make in this arena of reconciliation?

Chapter Five: Forgiveness: It's in Our DNA

1. Do you believe that forgiveness is really possible in the most traumatic experiences, or is this just a nice Christian saying?

2. What does it mean to say that forgiveness is in the DNA of every Christian?

3. Why isn't forgiveness an automatic response for Christians in light of our gratitude for God forgiving our burden of sin?

4. What is the implication of the statement that forgiveness is a decision of the will and not a feeling?

5. What are the things that have happened to you around the issue of race that you need to forgive?

6. What are the things that you need to receive forgiveness for around the issue of race?

Chapter Six: Tear Down This Wall!

1. It's easy to walk past people without making eye contact or speaking. How can doing something as simple as pausing to see the other and speak make a significant difference?

2. If calling a person by name communicates respect and acceptance, how can you put this simple practice into action?

3. We can make significant progress by learning each other's stories. What steps will you take to sensitize yourself to "life on the other side"?

4. Talk about the demographics where you live. Are they changing? If so, what is your attitude about the change?

Chapter Seven: God Don't Want No Coward Soldiers

1. Why is it important for us to keep the stories of heroes of the faith and heroes of reconciliation in front of us?

2. Do you see yourself as someone who is engaged in the battle for reconciliation? Why or why not?

3. Wilberforce introduced more than twenty resolutions to end slavery before finally achieving his goal. Does this encourage or discourage you? What does it teach us about commitment?

4. Martin Luther King Jr.'s commitment cost him his life. Do you think this fight for reconciliation is worth that much? Why or why not?

5. What points of application can you take away from the examples of Bill Pannell, Tom Skinner, Vernon Grounds, Paul Jewitt, and George McKinney?

6. Are there other names you would add to this Hall of Faith? Share them.

7. Dr. Perkins says that our children and their children are depending on each of us to do our part until the work is finally finished. What legacy are you leaving to your children in the arena of reconciliation?

8. What are the things that God is calling you to do to engage actively in this battle?

Chapter Eight: Prayer, The Weapon of Our Warfare

1. Why is it important to understand how Satan is involved in the battle for reconciliation?

2. Social activists have been blamed for not praying enough. Evangelicals have been blamed for not doing enough. How can we make sure that this is not what happens moving forward?

3. Dr. Perkins suggests that we should pray prayers that are so big that only God could accomplish them. What would be your request of God in this area of biblical reconciliation?

4. What are your own personal heart issues that need to be placed on the altar in the area of reconciliation?

5. What is your prayer for those who don't look like you?

6. Matthew 13:58 says that Jesus did not do many mighty works in Nazareth because of the unbelief of the people. How important is faith as we pray for the Lord to help us become reconciled to one another?

Chapter Nine: The Greatest of These Is Love

1. What is the connection between the love of God and reconciliation in the body of Christ?

2. Agape love is totally selfless and "does not change whether the love is returned or not." How many of your relationships are governed by this type of love?

3. Dr. Perkins talks about trying to outdo his friends by loving them more than they love him. Do you have friendships that are like this? Why or why not?

4. The African proverb suggests that people who seem like monsters because we view them from a distance can actually become friends if we get closer. Can you share a personal experience that has demonstrated this?

5. Dr. Perkins was able to make friends out of those who had opposing views by talking about what they both could agree on. How does this shed light on how opposite sides can approach the issue of reconciliation?

6. The relationship between Dr. Perkins and Wayne grew because they were able to recognize the differing strengths that the other brought to the table. What can we learn and apply from this?

7. Discuss the aspects of Wayne's interaction that demonstrated his love. How might this be instructive in building cross-cultural relationships?

CONTRIBUTING PASTORS

Dr. Mark DeYmaz

A thought-leading author, pastor, and recognized champion of the Multiethnic Church Movement, Mark planted the Mosaic Church of Central Arkansas in 2001, where he continues to serve as Directional Leader. In 2004, he co-founded the Mosaix Global Network with Dr. George Yancey and today serves as its president, and convener of the triennial National Multi-ethnic Church Conference. In 2008, he launched Vine and Village and remains active on the board of this 501(c)(3) nonprofit focused on the spiritual, social, and financial transformation of Little Rock's University District and the 72204 ZIP Code.

Mark is an adjunct professor at Gordon-Conwell Theological Seminary and teaches DMin courses at seminaries across the country including TEDS, Western, and Phoenix, where he earned his own DMin. in 2006. He and his wife, Linda, have been married for thirty years, reside in Little Rock, AR, and have four adult children and two grandchildren.

Albert Tate

Albert is a gifted and dynamic communicator who is passionate about sharing the gospel of Jesus Christ with the local and global church. Albert presents the gospel to people across the country in academic, retreat, and conference settings combining humor and storytelling of God's amazing grace and love. His unique and passionate style from the pulpit combines inspiration and challenge, laughter and tears as people are engaged at their core. His hope for Fellowship Monrovia is to cultivate a community of disciples that is unleashed to live out the Gospel by growing in a life of worship, gathering in community, and giving their lives away on mission.

Albert serves on the Board of Trustees at Azusa Pacific University and Fuller Youth Institute. He is married to the love of his life, LaRosa Tate, who he calls God's gift of amazing grace in his life. Together they have three beautiful children, Zoe, Bethany, and Isaac.

Dan Carroll

In 1987, Pastor Carroll began teaching a men's Bible study. For three years the study grew in scope and depth; and the families of the men involved began to come together. In 1989, Danny and his family went to the Youth With a Mission training school in Kona, Hawaii. They were introduced to cross-cultural ministry in Penang, Malaysia, where Danny received a vision for the world. After returning to the United States in 1990, Danny was encouraged by the men of the Bible study and their families to plant a church. This became Water of Life Community Church, where he is currently the senior pastor.

He holds multiple degrees, a BA in Religion from the University of La Verne, a MA in Education from the Claremont Graduate University, a MA in Christian Ministry from the International School of Theology, and a DMin from The King's Seminary. He and his wife, Gale, have been married for thirty-nine years and have two children, Shane and Katie, and three grandsons.

Dr. Eric Mason

Dr. Eric Mason, aka "Pastor E," is the founder and pastor of Epiphany Fellowship in Philadelphia, Pennsylvania. After more than two decades of gospel ministry, Dr. Mason has become known for his unquenchable passion to see the glory of Jesus Christ robustly and relevantly engaged in broken cities with the comprehensive gospel. Urban ministry is the heartbeat of his ministry and calling.

He is the founder and president of Thriving, an urban resource organization committed to developing leaders for ministry in the urban context. He is the recipient of multiple earned degrees, including a BS in psychology from Bowie State University, a Master of Theology from Dallas Theological Seminary, and a doctoral degree from Gordon-Conwell Theological Seminary. Dr. Mason has served as an adjunct professor at the College of Biblical Studies in Houston, Texas, and Biblical Theological Seminary outside of Philadelphia.

He and his wife, Yvette, have three sons, Immanuel, Nehemiah, and Ephraim, as well as one living daughter, Amalyah.

NOTES

Chapter 1: The Church Should Look Like That

1. http://www.ushistory.org/declaration/document/.
2. Julie Zauzmer, "What Happened When a Black and White Church Merged in Florida," *Washington Post*, February 7, 2017, https://www.washingtonpost.com/local/social-issues/two-fla-churches--one-black-one-white--merge-in-racial-reconciliation-effort/2017/02/07/a95dde72-e287-11e6-a547-5fb9411d332c_story.html?utm_term=.2d2175c54172.
3. Michael Clifford, in "The Making of One Church with Two Locations" (video), in H.B. Charles, "The Making of Shiloh Church of Orange Park," H.B. Charles Jr., November 24, 2014, https://www.hbcharlesjr.com/2014/11/24/the-making-of-shiloh-church-of-orange-park/.
4. This quote, often attributed to Blaise Pascal, is actually a paraphrase based on something he wrote in *Pensées*.

Chapter 2: One Race, One Blood

1. James Weldon Johnson, "The Creation," Poets.org, 1945, https://www.poets.org/poetsorg/poem/creation.
2. Dave Unander, *Shattering the Myth of Race* (Valley Forge, PA: Judson, 2000), 2.
3. Norman Anthony Peart, *Separate No More* (Grand Rapids: Baker, 2000), 97.
4. David T. Olson, *The American Church in Crisis* (Grand Rapids: Zondervan, 2008),18.
5. "Evangelical Leaders Agree on Racial Reconciliation," *National Association of Evangelicals*, February 2016, https://www.nae.net/evangelical-leaders-agree-racial-reconciliation/.
6. Bruce Gourley, "Yes, the Civil War was About Slavery," *Baptists and the American Civil War*, February 8, 2017 http://civilwarbaptists.com/featured/slavery/.
7. "What Nation's Largest Church Denomination Does for Racial Reconciliation After Painful Year," *Christian Broadcast News*, February 11, 2017, http://www1.cbn.com/cbnnews/us/2017/february/what-nations-largest-church-denomination-does-for-racial-reconciliation-after-painful-year.

8. David Roach, "H.B. Charles to Be Pastor's Conf. Nominee," *Baptist Press*, May 11, 2017, http://www.bpnews.net/48848/hb-charles-to-be-pastors-conf-nominee.

Living It Out: Mosaic Church, Little Rock

1. Mark DeYmaz, *Building a Healthy Multi-ethnic Church: Mandate, Commitments, and Practices of a Diverse Church* (San Francisco: Jossey-Bass/Leadership Network, 2007).
2. To learn more about Mosaic, visit www.mosaicchurch.net.
3. For a complete description and breakdown of Mosaic's ministry philosophy and measurable results over the past fifteen years, see *Disruption: Repurposing the Church to Redeem the Community* by Mark DeYmaz (Nashville: Thomas Nelson/Leadership Network, 2017).
4. *Our Finest Hour* was the theme of the third National Multi-ethnic Church Conference (November 2016, Dallas, TX), a triennial event facilitated by the Mosaix Global Network. To learn more about how Mosaix can assist you and your church in becoming multiethnic and disruptive, visit www.mosaix.info.
5. "It's not nice, it's necessary" is a phrase often repeated and first coined concerning the multiethnic church by Dr. David Anderson, founding pastor of Bridgeway Community Church in Columbia, MD.

Chapter 3: A Lament for Our Broken Past

1. Henri Nouwen, *Can You Drink the Cup?* (Notre Dame, IN: Ave Maria Press, 2006), 63.
2. "The Way of Lament," *Ligonier Ministries*, http://www.ligonier.org/blog/way-lament/.
3. Michael Card, *A Sacred Sorrow* (Colorado Springs: NavPress, 2005), 31–32, 86.
4. Rebecca Van Noord, "A Conversation with Hip Hop Artist and Preacher, Trip Lee," *Bible Study Magazine* (July/August 2017): 17–18.
5. Michael Lee, "Race and Ethnicity," *Christianity Today*, July 10, 2017, http://www.christianitytoday.com/edstetzer/2017/july/race-and-ethnicity.html.
6. Tony Evans, *Oneness Embraced* (Chicago: Moody, 2011), 139.
7. Steve Corbett and Brian Fikkert, *When Helping Hurts* (Chicago: Moody, 2009), 151.
8. Doug Banister, "Rethinking the $3,000 Missions Trip," *Red Letter Christians*, https://www.redletterchristians.org/rethinking-the-3000-missions-trip/.
9. Martin Luther King Jr., *Where Do We Go From Here: Chaos or Community?* (Boston: Beacon Press, 2010), 191.
10. D. L. Mayfield, "Covering Our Legacy of Lynching," *Christianity Today*, vol. 61, no. 7 (September 2017): 34.

Chapter 4: The Healing Balm of Confession

1. Dr. Mark DeYmaz, "The Multi-ethnic Church: a Biblical Mandate," Mosaic Church of Central Arkansas, http://www.dreamofdestiny .com/wp-content/uploads/2016/02/DeYmaz.TuesPm.ppt, citing David T. Olson, The American Church Research Project.
2. "Hate Is 'Alive Every Single Day,' LeBron James Says After Racist Graffiti Incident," National Public Radio, June 1, 2017, http://www .npr.org/sections/thetwo-way/2017/06/01/531023588/hate-is-living-every-day-lebron-james-says-after-racist-graffiti-incident.
3. John Piper, "Waiting for and Hastening the Day of Multiethnic Beauty," in Letters to a Birmingham Jail, ed. Bryan Loritts (Chicago: Moody, 2014), 57–73.
4. Ibid.
5. Peggy McIntosh, "White Privilege and Male Privilege" (Wellesley College Center for Research on Women: Wellesley, MA, 1988).
6. Eliza Berman, "Race in America," Time, April 30, 2015, http://time .com/3841969/split-screen-video-race-in-america/.
7. Henry Louis Gates, "How Many Slaves Landed in the US?," The Root, http://www.theroot.com/how-many-slaves-landed-in-the-us-1790873989.
8. Paul J. Pastor, "Efrem Smith Right-Side-Up-Side-Down," Outreach Magazine (May/June, 2017): 81–87.
9. "PCA GA: Overture 43 on Racial Reconciliation Approved 861-123," The Aquila Report, June 24, 2016, http://theaquilareport.com/ pca-ga-overture-43-on-racial-reconciliation-approved-861-123/.

Chapter 5: Forgiveness: It's in Our DNA

1. Meg Wagner, "As Trial Against Dylann Roof begins, Families of Charleston Church Shooting Victims Still Show Mercy," New York Daily News, November 3, 2016, http://www.nydailynews.com/news/ national/s-church-shooting-victims-families-forgive-dylann-roof-article-1.2855446.
2. "Charleston Shooting Cover Story," Time, http://time.com/ time-magazine-charleston-shooting-cover-story/.
3. "Amish Grace and Forgiveness," Lancaster, PA blog, https://lancaster pa.com/amish/amish-forgiveness/.
4. Joanna Walters, "The Happening: 10 Years After the Amish Shooting," The Guardian, October 2, 2016, https://www.theguardian.com/ us-news/2016/oct/02/amish-shooting-10-year-anniversary-pennsyl vania-the-happening.
5. Ibid.
6. Desmond Tutu, "Let South Africa Show the World How to Forgive," https://www.sol.com.au/kor/19_03.htm.
7. "Guideposts Classics: Corrie ten Boom on Forgiveness," Guideposts, https://www.guideposts.org/better-living/positive-living/guide-posts-classics-corrie-ten-boom-on-forgiveness.

8. Miroslav Volf, *Free of Charge: Giving and Forgiving in a Culture Stripped of Grace* (Grand Rapids: Zondervan, 2005), 159.

9. Nancy Leigh DeMoss, *Choosing Forgiveness* (Chicago: Moody, 2008), 59.

10. "Guideposts Classics: Corrie ten Boom on Forgiveness," *Guideposts*.

Chapter 6: Tear Down this Wall!

1. Suzanne Niles, "Director Jon Erwin Shares the Amazing True Story Behind 'Woodlawn,'" Sonoma Christian Home, October 28, 2015, https://sonomachristianhome.com/2015/10/director-jon-erwin-shares-the-amazing-true-story-behind-woodlawn/.

2. Ronald Reagan, "Remarks on East-West Relations at the Brandenburg Gate in West Berlin," Reagan Foundation, June 12, 1987, https://www.reaganfoundation.org/media/128814/brandenburg.pdf.

3. Dave Stone, "Tearing Down Walls: Tearing Down Racism," Southeast Christian Church, August 16, 2015, https://www.southeastchristian.org/sermons/tearing-down-walls/tearing-down-racism/.

4. Arthur Delaney and Alissa Scheller, "Who Gets Food Stamps? White People, Mostly," *Huffington Post*, February 28, 2015, http://www.huffingtonpost.com/2015/02/28/food-stamp-demographics_n_6771938.html.

5. J. D. Vance, *Hillbilly Elegy* (New York: HarperCollins, 2016), 3.

6. "The Help," CliffNotes, https://www.cliffsnotes.com/literature/h/the-help/summary-and-analysis/chapters-1718.

7. "Textbook Passage Referring to Slaves as Workers Prompts Outcry," *The Guardian*, Oct. 5, 2015, https://www.theguardian.com/education/2015/oct/05/mcgraw-hill-textbook-slaves-workers-texas.

8. Soong-Chan Rah, *Many Colors* (Chicago: Moody, 2010), 131.

9. "Sankofa," *The Evangelical Covenant Church* website, http://www.covchurch.org/justice/racial-righteousness/sankofa/.

10. Berea College, "The Power of Sankofa: Know History," *Carter G. Woodson Center*, https://www.berea.edu/cgwc/the-power-of-sankofa/.

11. Soong-Chan Rah, *Many Colors*, 125.

12. Gordon W. Allport, *The Nature of Prejudice* (Basic Books: New York, 1979), 281.

13. Rosalind Bentley, "After Philando Castile, 2 Churches in Roswell Seek Racial Reconciliation," *Atlanta Journal Constitution*, July 20, 2017, http://www.myajc.com/news/local/after-philando-castile-churches-roswell-seek-racial-reconciliation/LxogSTJP6J4iB05CJXEbcO/.

14. "Gentrification," *Urban Dictionary*, June 20, 2006, http://www.urbandictionary.com/define.php?term=Gentrification.

15. Bryan Loritts, "More on Leaving White Evangelicalism: A Response from Bryan Loritts," *Christianity Today*, October 2017, www.christianitytoday.com/edstetzer/2017/october/response-to-ray-changs-open-letter-to-john-piper.html.

16. Jim Barnes, "Sterling Church Sells Property, Chooses to Remain in Office Building and Focus on Ministry," *Washington Post*, June 9, 2014, https://www.washingtonpost.com/local/sterling-church-sells-property-chooses-to-remain-in-office-building-and-focus-on-ministry/2014/06/06/d94f149a-eb61-11e3-9f5c-9075d5508f0a_story.html?utm_term=.71a4935ef19d..

17. Ibid

18. Edward Gilbreath, "Breaking the Silence," *Covenant Companion*, November 6, 2017, http://covenantcompanion.com/2017/11/06/breaking-the-silence/.

Chapter 7: God Don't Want No Coward Soldiers

1. "Wesley to Wilberforce," *Christianity Today*, http://www.christianitytoday.com/history/issues/issue-2/wesley-to-wilberforce.html.

2. Ibid.

3. "Elijah Parish Lovejoy: 'A Martyr on the Altar of American Liberty,'" *Alton Web*, http://www.altonweb.com/history/lovejoy/.

4. Ibid.

5. Martin Luther King Jr., "Letter from a Birmingham Jail," April 16, 1963, in *Letters to a Birmingham Jail*, ed. Bryan Loritts (Chicago: Moody, 2014), 22.

6. Clayborne Carson and Kris Shepard, eds., *A Call to Conscience: The Landmark Speeches of Dr. Martin Luther King, Jr.* (New York: Grand Central Publishing, 2002), 211.

7. Lauralee Farrer, "This Is Then, That Was Now," Fuller Studio, 2014, https://fullerstudio.fuller.edu/this-is-then-that-was-now/.

8. Ibid.

9. James Earl Massey, "The Unrepeatable Tom Skinner," *Christianity Today*, vol. 38, no. 10, September 12, 1994, http://www.christianitytoday.com/ct/1994/september12/4ta011.html.

10. This phrase was coined by Rev. Samuel Hines and was used by Tom Skinner and many of his contemporaries when speaking of reconciliation. https://www.anderson.edu/uploads/sot/gilbert-lozano-response.pdf.

11. Paul Borthwick, *How to Be a World-Class Christian: Becoming Part of God's Global Kingdom* (Colorado Springs, Authentic, 2009), 118.

12. Lori Arnold, *Christian Examiner: San Diego County Edition*, "Golden Service: Bishop George D. McKinney and St. George Cathedral," vol. 30, no. 8 (August 2012): 1, 6, 8.

13. Soong-Chan Rah, "In Whose Image: The Emergence, Development, and Challenge of African-American Evangelicalism," (doctorate dissertation, Duke University, 2016), 180–252.

14. Scott Wenig, "A Man for All Evangelicals," *Christianity Today*, vol. 54, no. 11, http://www.christianitytoday.com/ct/2010/november/24.50.html?start=3.

15. "Chicago Declaration of Evangelical Concern," *Evangelicals for Social Action*, 1973, http://www.evangelicalsforsocialaction.org/about-esa/history/chicago-declaration-of-evangelical-social-concern/.

Chapter 8: Prayer, the Weapon of Our Warfare

1. Sherry L. Abbott, "My Mother Could Send up the Most Powerful Prayer: The Role of African American Slave Women in Evangelical Christianity" (master's thesis, University of Maine, 2003), 50.
2. Adapted from *"Thou, Dear God": Prayers That Open Hearts and Spirits*, The Reverend Doctor Martin Luther King, Jr., edited by Lewis V. Baldwin (Boston: Beacon Press, 2014), 97.
3. Mary McLeod Bethune, "Symphony of Life," quoted in James P. Moore Jr., *The Treasury of American Prayer* (New York: Doubleday, 2008), http://www.beliefnet.com/faiths/prayer/2009/01/prayers-from-african-americans-in-history.aspx?p=6.
4. Philip Amerson, "Will, Warren and the Klan," Philip Amerson blog, August 14, 2017, https://philipamerson.com/2017/08/14/will-warren-and-the-klan/.
5. Tony Evans, *Kingdom Prayer* (Chicago: Moody, 2016), 131–32.

Chapter 9: The Greatest of These Is Love

1. David Nelmes, "God is Agape Love," November 10, 2007, http://www.ezilon.com/articles/articles/7675/1/God-is-Agape-Love.
2. Eugene Peterson, *Leap Over a Wall* (New York: HarperCollins Publishers, 1997), 53.
3. Evelyn Bence, *Mornings with Henri J. M. Nouwen* (Cincinnati: Servant Publishing, 2005), 18.
4. Spencer Lewerenz and Barbara Nicolosi, *Behind the Screen: Hollywood Insiders on Faith, Film, and Culture* (Grand Rapids: Baker, 2001), 50.

Epilogue

1. Arno Michaelis, "I Learned the Hard Way How to Stop Hate," CNN Opinion, August 15, 2017, http://www.cnn.com/2017/08/15/opinions/ex-white-power-compassion-answer-michaelis-opinion/index.html.

Appendix: Chicago Declaration of Evangelical Social Concern (1973)

1. "Chicago Declaration of Evangelical Concern," *Evangelicals for Social Action*, 1973, http://www.evangelicalsforsocialaction.org/about-esa/history/chicago-declaration-of-evangelical-social-concern/.

ACKNOWLEDGMENTS

I am forever grateful to

... the multitude of friends whom God has given me along the way. Without them I would not be who I am today. The space on this page is not sufficient to list them all by name; but each one has inspired me in this journey and helped me remain faithful to His call.

... the CCDA movement and all of those persons who will catch the vision and link arms to advance His kingdom on earth. Stay in the battle until the fight is finished, and the victory is won.

... all the congregations that have so embraced me and the vision for the multicultural church. You have encouraged me to not come off the wall, even in the winter of life.

... my multicultural pastor friends who contributed to this book, Mark, Albert, Eric, and Dan. Thank you for lending your stories to this project. May God continue to bless the work of your hands.

... my longtime friend Shlomo Brabham, for his sharp eyes that helped perfect this message and for his enduring support.

... and to Moody Publishers. I am grateful for your vision for this project. You were determined that this manifesto needed to be written. Thank you Randall, Duane, and Karen for helping craft this message. This has truly been a labor of love. May God use this as a tool to help the church get unstuck.

ABOUT THE AUTHORS

John M. Perkins

John M. Perkins is cofounder of the Christian Community Development Association and director of the John and Vera Mae Perkins Foundation for Reconciliation, Justice, and Christian Community Development in Jackson, Mississippi. He is the author of many books, including *Let Justice Roll Down*, which was named by *Christianity Today* as one of the top fifty books that have shaped evangelicals.

Karen Waddles

Karen Waddles is a graduate of DePaul University and is completing a MASF at Moody Theological Seminary. She is a contributing writer to *Our Voices: Issues Facing Black Women in America* (Moody Publishers), *The Women of Color Study Bible* (Nia Publishing), and the *Sisters in Faith Devotional Bible* (Thomas Nelson).

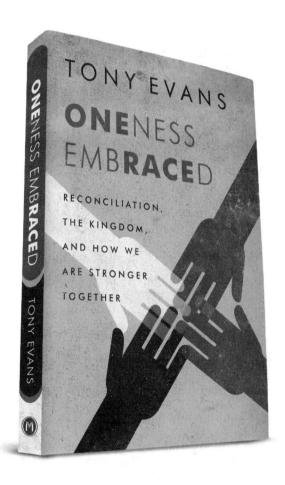

HOW TO ALLEVIATE POVERTY WITHOUT HURTING THE POOR . . . AND YOURSELF

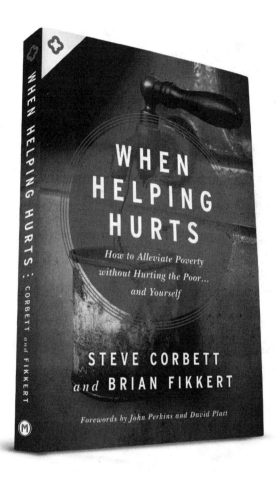

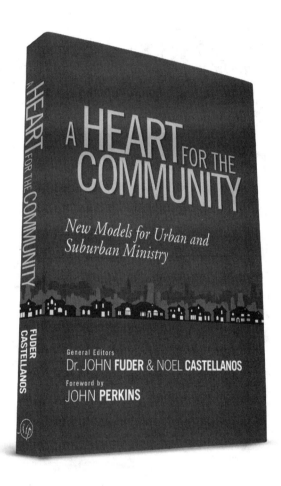